SPEAKER'S PROCESSION, HOUSE OF COMMONS

National Film Board

DEMOCRATIC GOVERNMENT *in* CANADA

ROBERT MacGREGOR DAWSON
M.A., D.Sc. (Econ.)

THE UNIVERSITY OF MINNESOTA PRESS
MINNEAPOLIS

BY THE SAME AUTHOR

The Principle of Official Independence
The Civil Service of Canada
Constitutional Issues in Canada, 1900-31
The Development of Dominion Status, 1900-36
The Government of Canada

[1050]

Copyright, Canada, 1949, by the University of Toronto Press. Printed and bound in Canada by the Copp Clark Co. Limited, Toronto.

Preface

THIS small book has been written to meet an obvious need in Canada and elsewhere—a short, descriptive account of Canadian government, national, provincial, and municipal. Many people have not the time nor, perhaps, the desire to read long and detailed discussions on what may at first appear to be an uninspiring subject; yet a substantial number are frequently anxious to know more about the fundamental ideas and structure of their government if it can be given in reasonably concise form. This book is designed to supply some of this information and understanding. To achieve this, it necessarily does more than provide a bald description of machinery and formal procedures. It is to the political behaviour of the human beings who are actively concerned that political science owes its major interest, its fascinating variety, and its inescapable complexity. Some glimpse of this more colourful human aspect will, I trust, be obtained from these pages.

The assistance which I received in preparing my *Government of Canada* has obviously been of great use in writing this book as well, and I wish to repeat the acknowledgments which occur in that volume. One name, however, must be added to the early list, namely, that of Professor K. G. Crawford, who gave substantial help in the preparation of the chapter on Municipal Government.

R. MacG. Dawson

"I see in the not remote distance one great nationality bound, like the shield of Achilles, by the blue rim of ocean. I see it quartered into many communities, each disposing of its internal affairs, but all bound together by free institutions, free intercourse and free commerce. . . . I see a generation of industrious, contented, moral men, free in name and in fact—men capable of maintaining, in peace and in war, a constitution worthy of such a country."

THOMAS D'ARCY MCGEE
May 2, 1860

Contents

I	The Canadian Democracy	3
II	The Canadian Constitution	17
III	The Distribution of Power	25
IV	Dominion-Provincial Finance	31
V	The Governor-General	37
VI	The Cabinet	41
VII	The Civil Service and the Departments	51
VIII	The Senate	62
IX	The House of Commons: Representation and Personnel	69
X	The House of Commons: Legislation	77
XI	The House of Commons and the Cabinet	85
XII	The Judiciary	95
XIII	Provincial Government	102
XIV	Municipal Government	116
XV	Political Parties	121
	APPENDICES	131
	BIBLIOGRAPHY	183
	INDEX	185

DEMOCRATIC GOVERNMENT IN CANADA

CHAPTER ONE

The Canadian Democracy

ONE of the fundamental assumptions underlying any democracy is that its nature and functions are understood by its own citizens; for only by having some grasp of its essentials can the body of citizens hope to make it work successfully. "That which most contributes to the permanence of constitutions", wrote Aristotle, "is the adaptation of education to the form of government. . . . The best laws, though sanctioned by every citizen of the state, will be of no avail unless the young are trained by habit and education in the spirit of the constitution." It is the "spirit of the constitution" which is the subject of this opening chapter, that is to say, the basic conceptions which give Canadian government its own special character. The remaining chapters will show in greater detail the nature and working of the structure which embodies these conceptions—the institutions used, the laws and customs observed, and the relationships which arise within and around the frame of government.

DEMOCRATIC GOVERNMENT

The first and most important characteristic of Canadian government is that it is a democracy, a government which is controlled by the greater part of the people. It rests on the will of the people and is at all times responsive to their opinions. It exists to serve the citizen and to provide him with a better life. It is *his* government, and the satisfaction of his wishes and his needs is the purpose for which it has been created. The government must therefore be constructed in such a form and its relationship to the citizen arranged in such a way that this primary aim can be realized. This will involve the counting of votes and the provision of other opportunities for finding out what the people want. It will also involve the maintenance of suitable facilities for discussion and deliberation. Provision will thus have to be made for such things as carefully designed methods and rules of discussion, the use and organization of committees, a way of obtaining accurate information and expert advice, a means of securing and using intelligent leadership. All these devices will help to ensure that the decisions of the democracy will be properly adapted to the wishes of the citizen.

But democratic government is more than a form of organization and more than cleverly designed machinery; it is also, as a Canadian Governor-General, Lord Tweedsmuir, once said, "a spiritual testament." It implies a number of vitally important beliefs and traditions which have been woven into the democratic fabric and have become quite inseparable from it. Among these are tolerance or a proper consideration for the opinions of others, freedom of discussion and criticism, freedom of religious beliefs, a respect for law, a regard for the rights of both the majority and the various minority groups into which the people are divided. Thus while it is true that, generally speaking, the wishes of the majority must prevail and the minorities must willingly accept the decisions of the majority, it is equally true that the minority also have certain rights, and there must be a corresponding willingness by the majority to recognize these rights as guaranteed. The degree to which this "willingness" is displayed is one of the distinguishing marks of modern governments. Autocratic or totalitarian governments simply refuse to tolerate dissenting groups or to allow any criticism of the policies of the government in power. Democratic governments not only permit such criticism, they even encourage it and provide in various ways for its free expression. A democracy will thus ensure certain basic rights and privileges to *all* its citizens—whether they belong to the majority or minority. All groups have a right to try to win support and adherents wherever they can find them. A minority today may thus become a majority tomorrow, and it is enabled by the casting of votes to have its turn at directing the government of the country and putting its policies into effect.

REPRESENTATIVE GOVERNMENT

The second characteristic of Canadian government is that it is founded on the representation of the great bulk of the people. The people in a democracy occasionally take their part in the government directly, that is, they may meet together and make their decisions themselves on the various matters which come before them. In ancient Greece, for example, the citizens of the Athenian democracy would assemble in the market place and transact in person all important public business. The same procedure is followed today in a few cantons in Switzerland and in certain small municipal districts in the United States. In some municipal governments in Canada the consent of the rate-payers to certain measures may be obtained directly by a special ballot or in a public meeting called for that particular purpose.

This method of arriving at decisions is, however, not common; for its effective use is largely confined to small groups which deal with relatively simple affairs. The much more usual method is for the people to act indirectly through others to whom they have delegated authority. "Representatives" are elected to speak and act for groups of voters in association with representatives who have been similarly chosen by voters in other areas in the nation. The Canadian House of Commons, the provincial legislatures, and the municipal councils are all composed of such representatives, elected by the people to act in their name and on their behalf.

The early Canadian colonies began with no representative institutions whatever. Quebec under French rule was governed by an appointed Council composed of the Governor, the Intendant, the Bishop, and other officials and citizens. The British colonies were ruled by a Governor (sent over from England) assisted by a Council which the Governor appointed. Indeed, in Newfoundland the Governor was even able for many years to dispense with a Council entirely. But representation soon followed the English settlement in Canada as it had in the early American colonies in the seventeenth and eighteenth centuries. The English people had long enjoyed a substantial measure of self-government at home. This right they brought with them across the Atlantic as one of their most cherished possessions, and they insisted on its speedy recognition in their new environment. Virginia, the earliest of the permanent settlements, was founded in 1607, and it obtained its first representative legislature in 1619. Halifax, the first permanent English settlement in what later became Canada, was founded in 1749, and Nova Scotia proceeded to elect its first Legislative Assembly only a few years later in 1758. A similar sequence of events followed the settlement of other colonies in Canada. Elected Legislative Assemblies were summoned with little delay[1] and they at once began to participate with the Governor and Council in conducting the affairs of the colonies.

RESPONSIBLE GOVERNMENT

Canadian government is not only representative, it is also responsible. It belongs with that large group which have followed the British model and which are variously known as cabinet, parliamentary, or responsible governments. The distinguishing feature of this group is the close relations which exist between the executive and legislative branches of the government, or, as they are called, the Cabinet and the Parliament. Thus the small body which initiates policies

---

[1]Representative Assemblies in each colony or province were first elected as follows: Nova Scotia, 1758; Prince Edward Island, 1773; New Brunswick, 1784; Upper and Lower Canada (Ontario and Quebec), 1791; Newfoundland, 1832; British Columbia, 1856; Manitoba, 1870; North-West Territories (Alberta and Saskatchewan), 1888.

and oversees the enforcement of the law—the executive—works in harmony with the much larger and essentially representative body—the legislature—which enacts the laws and exercises general deliberative, critical, and supervisory functions. To do this effectively, the Prime Minister and the other members of the Cabinet have seats in Parliament, and they lead and direct its activities. They are at all times "responsible" to the House of Commons and must resign if they cannot retain its support and confidence. In short, the Prime Minister and Cabinet must always have a majority of members in the House of Commons willing to help and vote for them, and their policies and those of the majority of members in the House must therefore be substantially the same at all times.

The United States furnishes an example of a democracy under a quite different system, which is usually known as presidential or congressional government. Here the executive, legislative, and judicial powers of government are separated from one another, and each is entrusted to a different person or group of persons. Each of these three authorities, moreover, is supposed to exercise its powers to a large degree apart from the others. Thus the President (and his Cabinet) are not allowed to sit in Congress; the President and the members of Congress are elected by different methods and hold their positions for a different term of years; neither is responsible to the other, nor can one of them compel the resignation of the other because of loss of confidence or a lack of sympathy with its policies or measures. Such an arrangement gives permanence and security to the President, for his independence of Congress allows him to stay in office for a fixed term. On the other hand, as a result of this separation, the President and Congress are rarely able to achieve the same degree of harmony and unity of purpose which is obtained under the parliamentary system.

Responsible government did not appear in British North America as early as representation; indeed, ninety years separated the first assembly in Canada from the first responsible Cabinet. During this transitionary period (which varied somewhat from colony to colony) the representatives of the people in the Legislative Assembly took some part in the government, but they were not the masters of it. The executive power was in the hands of the Governor and his appointed assistants, called the Executive Council; while the elected Assembly shared the legislative power with a companion body, the Legislative Council (appointed by the Governor), as well as with the Governor himself, who had to assent to legislation. The people had therefore only the one body, the Legislative Assembly, under their control; the three others, Governor, Executive Council, and Legislative Council, were largely independent of popular authority. The prolonged effort to change this undesirable condition is known in the history books as the "struggle for responsible government". It involved many quarrels in all the colonies affected and became actual rebellion in Upper and Lower Canada in 1837. The result was the investigation and report by Lord Durham in 1838-9 which endorsed the principles of responsible government. The system he proposed was eventually adopted in 1848.

The responsibility of the Cabinet to the people's representatives in the legislature is enforced (as stated above) by a vote of the legislative members, some of them voting in favour of the Cabinet, some opposing it. When such a vote goes against the Cabinet, it resigns and makes way for a new Cabinet, which, in turn, must be able to obtain the support of a majority of the representatives. In January, 1848, the Cabinet in Nova Scotia was changed under these circumstances, and six weeks later a similar vote brought about a change of Cabinets in the province of Canada. The Governor of Canada at this time was Lord Elgin, whose determination a year later to follow the advice of his Cabinet in assenting to the Rebellion Losses Bill led to rioting and the burning of the Parliament building in Montreal.

Representative government became by this change *responsible* government; and the genuine control of the people of Canada over their political institutions dates from that time. Other provinces in due course were able to adopt and follow the same practice.[1] An interesting fact concerning this extremely vital reform was that it was not necessary to pass a law to bring it into effect. The Governor was simply given instructions by the British Government to secure an Executive Council (or Cabinet) which would have the confidence of the Legislative Assembly; and all he did was to follow his instructions. Constitutional changes of first-rate importance are thus sometimes made easily and informally by the simple alteration of a custom—a practice which will be discussed again in later pages.

FEDERAL GOVERNMENT

A fourth characteristic is that the Canadian government is a federation. In some countries all the powers of government are concentrated in one central authority at the capital; and while other governments may exist in smaller geographical areas, these are created by the central authority and always operate under its direction. Thus in Great Britain the national government at Westminster is supreme; and while many county, city, and other local authorities exist, they derive their powers from the British Parliament and do their work under the general supervision of the national Cabinet.

A federation is differently organized and stands in striking contrast to the unitary government just described. In a federation the broad powers of government are distributed between a central or federal government on the one hand and a number of state or provincial governments on the other; and each exercises its own powers without being subordinate or inferior to the other. Thus in Canada (and in the

---

[1] Responsible government was introduced in the different provinces as follows: Nova Scotia, Canada (Ontario and Quebec), New Brunswick, 1848; Prince Edward Island, 1851; Newfoundland, 1855; British Columbia, Manitoba, 1871; North-West Territories (Alberta and Saskatchewan), 1897.

United States also) the federal or Dominion Parliament has power to deal with certain general or national topics, such as defence, post office, and railways; while the provincial legislatures deal with other topics of a more local nature, such as education, highways, and municipal government. Such a system is very complex and very difficult to keep running smoothly and efficiently; but it has the great advantage of permitting wide differences among the provincial units and thus for certain limited purposes allowing these units to follow whatever policies they consider best.

The Canadian federation[1] came into existence on July 1, 1867. Although the idea of union among the British North American colonies had been mentioned on many occasions, the momentous initial step was taken in 1864 by Nova Scotia, New Brunswick, and Prince Edward Island, who agreed to send delegates to Charlottetown to discuss a Maritime union. The province of Canada, moved by a variety of political and economic reasons, wished to propose a more comprehensive plan, and at its request its delegates were permitted to join the Charlottetown Conference and offer their proposals for consideration. The scheme for a larger union was accepted in general principle by the Conference, and another meeting was called in Quebec later in the year to pursue the matter further. To this meeting Newfoundland also sent delegates with a view to the possibility of making the union even more comprehensive than that originally proposed.

The Quebec Conference eventually agreed on seventy-two resolutions which outlined a federal form of government for the united provinces. While most of the delegates believed that a more centralized or unitary government would be preferable, they agreed that few provinces would accept such a proposal. A federation allowed both common action for many common purposes and provincial freedom in other

---

[1]The common word for this in Canada is Confederation, a term which, properly speaking, is applicable to a different form of organization, where the component states are really separate and independent and come together in what is an alliance rather than a union.

matters, a freedom which was sought by the Maritime Provinces and most of all by Quebec, where a different language, race, religion, law, and culture made a formal recognition of these differences inescapable. The delegates to the Quebec Conference were, however, greatly influenced by the civil war which had recently broken out in the United States and which they ascribed to excessively large state powers and insufficient authority in the American national government. They therefore planned a Canadian constitution which, though establishing a federation, nevertheless embodied a strong central authority working in association with provinces which exercised a selected list of powers regarded as appropriate for the smaller area.

The resolutions of the Quebec Conference met with a mixed reception. Prince Edward Island quickly rejected the proposed union, and Newfoundland, after a delay of some years, did the same. In New Brunswick, the Government which had helped draft them was thrown out of office, and in Nova Scotia, while the legislature at first took no action, the people were unmistakably hostile. The legislature of the province of Canada, however, gave the resolutions its formal approval; and eventually the legislatures of Nova Scotia and New Brunswick agreed to reconsider the proposals for federation at another conference in London. The conference between delegates from these three provinces and the British Government met in 1866 and proceeded to endorse with many amendments the earlier Quebec Resolutions. The London Resolutions (as they came to be known) then served as the basis for a bill which in due course passed the British Parliament as the British North America Act, 1867. This Act with some later amendments forms the present written constitution of Canada.

The four original provinces in the existing federation were thus Ontario, Quebec (the province of Canada being split in 1867 into Ontario and Quebec), Nova Scotia, and New Brunswick. Manitoba was created out of federal territory and was admitted as a province in 1870. British Columbia entered the federation in 1871; Prince Edward Island in 1873. Alberta and Saskatchewan had been, like Manitoba, part of the western territory, and they became provinces in 1905. Newfoundland entered as the tenth province in 1949.

THE RULE OF LAW

Another important feature of the government of Canada is its acceptance of the principle known as the rule or supremacy of law. This principle of the British law which came to Canada with the early settlers exists for the protection of the citizen against possible excesses of authority by government officials. It means that the government itself is controlled by the law and must operate according to its terms, that all acts of government must be based on a law and not on the whim or caprice of the officials who may happen to be in authority. A Prime Minister, or a customs inspector, or a policeman, is thus under the same legal compulsion to obey the law as the most humble citizen.

Nor, according to a proper regard for this principle, should the law give exceptionally generous discretionary powers to government officials; for if these officials exercise a free hand and a wide choice in making decisions, their powers will tend to be uncontrolled. Thus a government department which (let us suppose) is given a general power of issuing orders to preserve conditions of public health is under far less control than one which is told by the explicit terms of a law what conditions it can regulate and the extent and manner of that regulation. It is evident that when legal powers are granted —as they certainly must be granted to enable officials to carry out the purposes of Parliament—the statement which bestows these powers should be made, whenever possible, in "reasonably precise" terms. The citizen will in this way have some conception of the power which has been given and some assurance that the official will not and cannot act— even under the law—in an arbitrary manner.

The great difficulty today is that governments are now doing far more things than were dreamt of fifty years ago, and that many of these things are so complicated or of such a nature that government officials must be allowed to have greater powers of initiative and decision. To return to the above example of the preservation of public health. A modern government department is not content (as its predecessors were) to exercise a few simple functions concerning sanitation and quarantine. It establishes hospitals; it conducts research into medical problems of many kinds; it provides serums and medicines; it gives free physical examinations for the detection of such diseases as tuberculosis; it educates the people in matters of health by lectures and exhibitions; it inspects meat-packing and canning plants; it sets up standards to ensure the purity of foods, and analyses many products in order to make certain that these standards are maintained.

These activities are far too numerous and complex to be covered in detail by ordinary laws. They must therefore not only be entrusted in large measure to government officials (which is unavoidable in any event) but to government officials who are allowed to use their own judgment in carrying out the activities which the laws in fairly general terms impose on them. Despite this strong tendency, however, the principle of the rule of law, as stated above, is still fundamentally sound; and while its scope has been somewhat narrowed by modern necessities, it still remains a sturdy bulwark against abuse of power. The rule of law furnishes, indeed, a most striking contrast with those conditions which are found under a dictatorship; for autocratic rule will tolerate no effective restraint on the government itself or on its agents, and the citizen accordingly has no sure protection against the exercise of arbitrary and unpredictable authority.

THE INDEPENDENCE OF THE JUDICIARY

The chief guarantee which the citizen possesses that the supremacy of law will be maintained is his right of appeal to the courts for protection, coupled with the assurance that he will there be sure of finding justice. The courts, when disputes are brought before them for decision, will scrutinize alleged breaches of the law and will be prepared to intervene and protect the citizen against any infraction of his legal rights. The liberty of the citizen thus depends in the last resort upon the courts. Their efficacy rests in turn upon the uprightness and impartiality of the judiciary and its freedom from any control by the executive or legislature which might conceivably endeavour to interfere with its work. Hence the sixth characteristic of Canadian government is found in the independence of the judiciary, another part of the priceless political heritage which Canada has received from England. It has already been pointed out that the division of powers is not observed in Canada as applied to the legislature and the executive, but that Parliament and Cabinet are continually kept in very close relationship with each other. Canadian government does recognize, however, a division of powers between these two authorities and the judiciary, so that the judges are able to perform their delicate functions without any fear of intimidation or control by Cabinet or Parliament. The means which are used to obtain this independence of the judiciary will be discussed later; it is sufficient here to observe that the Canadian citizen has no cause to fear that his complaints against his government will not be fairly heard and decided, or that the judge who tries his case will be exposed to any sinister pressure from the legislative or executive branch of the government.

CANADA AND THE BRITISH COMMONWEALTH

The last characteristic of Canadian government is that Canada is a sovereign independent state associated with others of equal status in the British Commonwealth of Nations. The gradual attainment of this position from one of early complete subordination to Great Britain has been a history filled with incident and dotted with constitutional issues of major and minor importance. Control over most internal affairs—matters which arise within national boundaries—followed closely upon the winning of responsible government a century ago; control over external affairs—peace, war, the relations with other countries, and so forth—is much more recent and followed speedily upon the events of the First World War.

The decisive step in this modern period was taken in 1926 when an Imperial Conference (composed of representatives of Great Britain, the self-governing Dominions, and India) issued a formal statement on the constitutional relations of members of the British Commonwealth. It declared that Great Britain and the Dominions were "equal in status, in no way subordinate one to another in any aspect of their domestic or external affairs, though united by a common allegiance to the Crown." The position of Canada and other Dominions was further clarified in 1931 by the passage of the Statute of Westminster, which removed most of the legal inequalities which still persisted.

Events before, during, and after the Second World War carried these developments even further, though two traces of the earlier relationship survived. Thus Canada must still go to the Imperial Parliament to secure an amendment to her formal constitution, and in many legal disputes an appeal was until very recently taken to England to the highest Commonwealth court, the Judicial Committee of the Privy Council. In 1949, however, the Canadian Parliament stopped these appeals; and there is no doubt that the amending power will also be vested in a Canadian authority as soon as Canadians decide what other process of amendment they prefer. With this one exception (which in reality can scarcely be regarded as such) Canada is, in the full sense of the word, completely self-governing. She not only has absolute control over all matters within her borders, she declares war, makes peace, maintains her own armed forces, sends ambassadors and ministers to foreign capitals, negotiates her own treaties, and is a member of the United Nations. She keeps, however, her membership in that unique political association, the British Commonwealth of Nations. She acknowledges with other members a common king, and consults and co-operates with them on terms of absolute equality, though she remains an independent nation and may leave the association whenever it may suit her purposes to do so. Such action appears to be most unlikely; for sentimental ties are strong, and the material advantages of membership in the Commonwealth are far from negligible. The British Commonwealth, moreover, may be justly regarded as the most successful experiment in international relations which has yet been made in human history. Its dissolution at a time when democratic nations are earnestly seeking a better understanding and closer co-operation with one another would be a retrograde step indeed, and one which at present, at least, does not appear to be desired by any considerable body of opinion in Canada.

CHAPTER TWO

The Canadian Constitution

THE constitution of Canada is not confined, as some people think, to the thirty-odd pages of the original British North America Act, or even to the Act and its amendments. Although undoubtedly a large section of the constitution is set forth in the Act and its amendments, other parts are found elsewhere and under a variety of forms: some written, some unwritten; some explicit, some extremely intangible and at times even uncertain. The chief categories into which the constitution may be divided are as follows: (1) the British North America Act (and its amendments); (2) custom or usage; (3) acts of the Canadian Parliament; (4) acts of the British Parliament; (5) judicial decision; (6) other forms.

1. *The British North America Act (and its amendments)*

This Act not only marked the beginning of the Canadian federation, it also stated many of the essential rules under which the new government was to function. The powers of the federal government; the powers of the provinces; the broad features of the executive, the judiciary, the Senate and the House of Commons; general provisions regarding the provincial governments and special provisions concerning Ontario and Quebec (which started them on their new provincial existence)—all these appear in the written clauses of the British North America Act. The amendments, which are still formally passed by the British Parliament, occupy the same basic constitutional position as the original Act.

A special variation of the normal amendment is composed of what might be called "constitutional statutes", which are acts passed by the Canadian Parliament that have substantially modified the British North America Act in accordance with powers granted by its own clauses. Thus the Saskatchewan Act and the Alberta Act (which created these provinces and admitted them to the federation), while nominally statutes of the Canadian Parliament, come very close to being in effect genuine amendments to the British North America Act itself. Moreover, once the Canadian Parliament has enacted one of these statutes, it has no legal power to change it.

2. *Custom or usage*

This is scarcely less essential than the provisions of the British North America Act. The government of Canada, like those of the colonies before federation, has always rested to a remarkable degree upon custom; that is, certain things have tended to be done in a certain way because they have been done in that way before. The origin of one of these customs in Canada has already been described, namely, the introduction of responsible government by the simple expedient of instructing a Governor to select his Cabinet from those members of the legislature who would be able to secure the support of the elected lower house. This was, of course, simply an adoption of the British custom under which the Sovereign chose the British Cabinet according to the same unwritten understanding; and the custom which was thus reproduced in Nova Scotia in 1848 has been consistently followed since then by both Dominion and provincial governments. This practice is not even mentioned in the British North America Act nor does it occur in any Canadian statute. Every Canadian, moreover, knows with certainty that if the Cabinet ceases to enjoy the support of the House of Commons it must either resign immediately or hold a general election. In the latter alternative, it must still resign (again by custom) if it is unable to command a majority of votes in the newly elected House. No part of the written constitution is any more firmly established than this cardinal principle, which rests on nothing more substantial than a generally accepted usage. It is, furthermore, the most important single fact about the government of Canada.

There are many other customary parts of the constitution, especially those which are concerned with the exercise of the powers of the Governor-General, the position and functions of the Prime Minister and the Cabinet and their relations to Parliament, and the system of political parties and the place they occupy in the government. A number of these will be noted in due course.

3. *Acts of the Canadian Parliament*

Many aspects of Canadian government are covered by the ordinary statutes which are enacted by Parliament from time to time. Some of these are of outstanding importance, such as the statute which created the Supreme Court of Canada or that which decides who shall be allowed to vote at elections; others deal with constitutional matters of relatively minor consequence. They are to be distinguished from the comparatively rare "constitutional statutes" (mentioned under (1) above) chiefly by the fact that they may be altered again at any time by the Canadian Parliament.

4. *Acts of the British Parliament*

In colonial days these used to occupy a very prominent place indeed, but years ago a constitutional usage developed whereby the British Parliament became very careful not to enact any laws which might be interpreted as an interference in Canadian affairs. Two exceptions, however, should be noted. British statutes were for many years made applicable to Canada in a few fields where it was desirable to have common legislation for the whole Empire; for example, the regulation of merchant shipping. Secondly, there was the British North America Act itself (and its amendments) which was, of course, an Act of the British Parliament.

The Statute of Westminster, 1931, not only confirmed and emphasized the general policy of the British Parliament abstaining from legislating on Canadian matters, it also provided explicitly that no future British statutes would apply to Canada unless Canada so desired. Past acts remained applicable to Canada, but these could be modified or repealed (so far as Canada was concerned) by the Canadian Parliament. The first of the above exceptions thus largely disappeared. The British North America Act, however, has remained in its dominant position, and it cannot even now be changed by the unaided efforts of the Canadian Parliament. This will be discussed presently in greater detail.

5. *Judicial decision*

The courts make a notable contribution to the Canadian constitution through their interpretation of the law in cases which are brought before them for decision. One aspect of this function involves the pronouncement by the courts on the validity of Dominion and provincial legislation which is enacted under the provisions of the British North America Act. If the courts decide that a statute of either the Dominion or provincial legislature has gone beyond the powers given that body by the supreme law, the British North America Act, they declare the statute void or *ultra vires* (beyond the powers of) that legislature; if it is within the powers so granted, the statute is declared valid or *intra vires*. This is no more than the application of the simple principle that no body can legally do any act which it is not legally competent to do. Inasmuch as the British North America Act is the source of all legislative power in Canada, both Dominion and province are necessarily limited by the power so given. The courts of law thus stand as an arbiter between rival Dominion and provincial authorities and they prevent encroachment on rival fields of jurisdiction, a most valuable function under a federal system where such conflicts are inevitable and unending.

A similar question of jurisdiction may arise in regard to the legal powers of other bodies. The Governor-General-in-Council may exceed the statutory powers which have been vested in it by Parliament, or a municipal authority may pass a by-law which exceeds the powers granted it by provincial statute, or either may transgress a section of the British North America Act. If the courts are satisfied that such a body has stepped outside the powers legally conferred on it, they will declare the order-in-council, by-law, or whatever it may be, to be *ultra vires*. All these constitutional interpretations, whether of jurisdiction or of the meaning to be placed on the words and phrases of a statute, are clearly almost as significant as the actual provisions of the British North America Act.

6. *Other forms*

The constitution takes other forms which need not be set down in detail here. The English common law which came to Canada (except Quebec) with the early settlement is an essential part of the constitution, especially as it affects the fundamental rights of the citizen, such as freedom of speech, freedom of assembly, the right to trial by jury. British orders-in-council still comprise a small part, and Canadian orders-in-council a much larger part of the constitution. The rules and privileges of Parliament make up another minor section; and there are still others.

CONSTITUTIONAL DEVELOPMENT

This complex constitution is, moreover, never stationary: it is always in process of change; and its composite nature suggests the variety of methods through which it is constantly developing. Customs will inevitably alter from time to time; Parliament will enact new or amending statutes; the courts of law never cease to pass judgment on disputes which come before them. Thus year by year, and almost day by day, the constitution grows and takes on new characteristics which in large measure spring out of the needs of the time. A few of these adaptations—especially the customary ones—may be almost unsuspected until they have become established and rooted by repetition. Even the specific terms of the British North America Act are subject to quiet transformation by judicial decision or by custom. The Act, for example, gives many powers to the Governor-General; but the building up of many precedents has had the effect of transferring the real exercise of these powers to the Cabinet. The Governor thus continues to perform his constitutional functions according to the law, but he does so while acting on the advice of his Cabinet, who assume the responsibility for what he does and defend it as their own act in the House of Commons. A most conscientious reading of the British North America Act, therefore, does not necessarily give an accurate picture of how Canadian government actually works. That knowledge must be extended and even substantially modified by an understanding of the other parts of the constitution.

FORMAL AMENDMENT

The British North America Act can be *formally* amended or altered only by an act of the British Parliament. But here, too, custom has become of vital importance; for by long-established precedent the British Parliament will not pass any amendment on its own initiative, but only after it has received a joint address passed by the Canadian Senate and House of Commons requesting that the desired amendment should be enacted. Can the Canadian Parliament, then, ask for any amendment it wishes? It frequently does so without reference to any other body; and there is no legal provision which prevents such procedure at any time. But mere legal provisions, as the above pages have indicated, are not necessarily decisive. In this matter of constitutional amendment the provinces are frequently deeply concerned and will have views which they will wish to have considered. One school of thought, indeed, insists that the original federation embodied a compact or agreement which cannot be altered except with the unanimous consent of all the provinces, and that the Canadian Parliament is therefore bound to obtain this consent before forwarding its request to Westminster. This "compact theory", however, has little legal or historical justification, though it is generally admitted that the Dominion Parliament does not and should not have an unfettered right of demanding any amendment it desires without any regard for provincial opinion. Thus most people would agree that an amendment which closely affects provincial rights and powers should not be requested by the Canadian Parliament unless the provinces have first been consulted and at least a substantial measure of provincial consent has been obtained.

One fact concerning the system of making amendments is indisputable: it is unsatisfactory as it now stands. But any single method that can be offered in its place at once encounters the fundamental difficulty which underlies this problem, namely, the need for a method of amendment which will be both elastic and inelastic, which will make the constitution in some respects easy to change, and in other respects virtually unchangeable. For while the written constitution should be able to yield to the pressure of fresh necessities and altering circumstances, it is also desirable that it should be able to resist pressure in those parts which deal with certain fundamental rights. Thus the section in the British North America Act which states the qualifications of a senator needs no special protection; but those sections which guarantee sectarian schools in some provinces and the use of the French and English languages in Quebec and the Dominion should be made virtually impregnable. The problem is not, however, hopeless; and proposals have been advanced which would establish different methods of amendment for different part of the constitutional Act. Such a plan would allow some sections of the Act to be amended by the Dominion Parliament alone while others could be amended by the

Dominion Parliament and the legislatures of two-thirds of the provinces. Sections such as those dealing with education and language could be specially entrenched behind an amending clause which would demand the consent of the Dominion Parliament and of the legislatures of all the provinces.

The Canadian people, however, have not yet been able to agree on this or any other method of making amendments to the British North America Act. Their indecision has been the chief cause of the British Parliament's continuing to retain a power which could logically have been assumed long ago by some Canadian authority. The British Parliament, for its part, is anxious to transfer its amending power at the earliest opportunity: it simply awaits a decision of the Canadian people as to what kind of amending clause they wish to have inserted in the Act. Once that is settled, the British Parliament will enact the desired amendment, and retire with some relief from what is now an ambiguous and thankless position.

HOUSE OF COMMONS IN SESSION *National Film Board*

CITIZENSHIP CEREMONY, SUPREME COURT, OTTAWA *National Film Board*

National Film Board

ADVISORY COMMITTEE, INDUSTRIAL PRODUCTION
CO-OPERATION BOARD, OTTAWA

National Film Board

DEPUTY MINISTER OF FISHERIES DISCUSSES
WHALING ON INSPECTION TOUR

CHAPTER THREE

The Distribution of Power

ONE of the outstanding characteristics of the government of Canada is its federal structure, the distribution of power between the Dominion on the one hand and the provinces on the other. The main purpose of this distribution is readily stated: to allocate all powers of government between the two types of governing authorities. The general principle to be applied is also clear: to give matters of broad national interest to the Dominion and matters of local or particular interest to the provinces. But the actual distribution and its day-to-day interpretation and application are extremely complicated, and it is this which makes the heaviest demands on the political sagacity, the tolerance, the administrative skill, and the goodwill of all parties to the relationship. The following account is admittedly over-simplified; but the lines of distribution are indicated and some little conception of the many accompanying difficulties may be discerned.

1. *Dominion powers*

The grant of powers to the federal Parliament is set forth for the most part in Section 91 of the British North America Act. The Dominion is here given a general power to enact "laws for the peace, order, and good government of Canada" on all subjects not given to the provinces, and this statement is followed by a list of twenty-nine powers as illustrations of the general power. A discussion of this "general" power appears below under item (5).

Many of the twenty-nine enumerated powers of the federal Parliament are known through experience by any Canadian.

Everyone is aware, for example, that the Dominion can borrow money; raise money by taxes ("any mode or system of taxation", to use the words of the Act); maintain armed forces; operate the postal service; appoint judges and other public officials; enact the criminal law; issue coinage; and take the census. Several other topics would probably come to mind after a little thought, such as, banks; legal tender; weights and measures; patents and copyrights; penitentiaries; naturalization; lighthouses, navigation, and shipping; railways and canals. If to these are added trade and commerce; fisheries; bills of exchange; and Indian affairs, the list becomes fairly complete.

2. *Provincial powers*

These appear in Section 92 of the Act. Here again, a Canadian should be able to name from his own experience a number of provincial fields—taxation; borrowing money on the credit of the province; public lands; municipal government; and local works and undertakings. To these the Act adds also other powers: the amendment of the provincial constitution (except for the office of Lieutenant-Governor); the establishment of provincial offices and appointments thereto; the maintenance of hospitals and similar institutions; the constitution, organization, and maintenance of provincial courts; the issuing of licences; the incorporation of companies with provincial objects; property and civil rights; and several others.

The provincial taxing power, it may here be noted, is limited to the levying of *direct* taxes only—those which in all likelihood cannot normally be passed on by the taxpayer to anyone else—whereas the Dominion taxing power is unlimited. Taxes on income, on estates of deceased persons, on the consumer of gasoline in proportion to the amount of gasoline consumed, are all examples of direct taxes, for they will almost certainly come out of the pockets of those from whom they are collected. Examples of *indirect* taxes (which cannot be imposed by the provinces) are customs duties of all kinds, and excise taxes on tobacco, spirituous liquors, and other luxuries. In most instances because these can be passed on, they are eventually paid by someone other than the one on whom they are first levied. It must be remembered, however, that inasmuch as the Dominion can raise money by "any mode or system of taxation" it may impose both direct and indirect taxes.

3. *Concurrent powers*

Both Dominion and provincial legislatures may enact laws relating to agriculture and immigration. If any part of the laws of the two authorities should conflict, the Dominion law prevails.

4. *Education*

The province is given exclusive power to make laws in relation to education provided it respects any right or privilege which anyone has by law in the province at the time of union, and provided that the Protestant or Roman Catholic minority has an appeal to the Governor-General-in-Council from any act or decision of any provincial authority affecting such rights or privileges which may exist or be later established in the province. The Governor-General-in-Council may order that remedial measures be taken, and, if necessary, the federal Parliament may enact legislation to carry out the provisions of this section. Under the terms of union with Newfoundland, however, any subsequent law of that province which may prejudicially affect any right or privilege with respect to denominational schools existing at the time of union is to be reviewed by the courts and not by the Governor-in-Council.

Even a careful reading of the above scheme of distribution gives little inkling of the bewildering conflicts and difficulties which lie hidden under what are apparently simple phrases. The conflict in taxation, which arises under the specific terms of the Act, is perhaps the easiest to interpret. Both Dominion and province may find themselves quite legitimately imposing *direct* taxes on the same object (notably in income and inheritance taxes), and while this may prove embarrassing, both taxes are valid. It was thus possible some years ago for a very wealthy man in one province to have to pay provincial and Dominion income taxes amounting to 105 per cent of his income.

Again, the apparent subject-matter of an act may not be a reliable test of its real purpose, which may be to invade a field of jurisdiction normally closed to the enacting authority. Thus a provincial law, which was nominally concerned with the imposition of a direct tax (a legitimate provincial power) on banks, has been set aside by the courts because it was in reality trying indirectly to control "banks and banking", a Dominion subject.

Difficulty may also arise in the interpretation of what is known as the "aspect" doctrine. The courts will allow a province to legislate on one aspect of a certain subject because it relates to a provincial power (such as "property and civil rights"), while at the same time they will also allow the Dominion to legislate on a different aspect of the same subject under one of its assigned powers (such as "criminal law"). Jurisdiction over a field has in this way often been split between the two authorities, thus making effective legislation and administration in such a field extremely difficult.

All these sources of conflict are mentioned here briefly (and with inadequate detail), but the mere statement of them will serve to indicate in some measure the complications which tend to blur the lines of demarcation between Dominion and provincial jurisdiction.

5. *Residual power*

No listing of separate powers can be so extensive and complete that it leaves none unsaid. Federal constitutions therefore use the device of naming some explicit powers in detail and then giving the balance or residue to either the federal or the provincial government. It will be recalled (see item (1) above) that the Dominion Parliament was given a general power to enact laws for the "peace, order, and good government of Canada"—that is, a general power of legislation—in relation to all matters not given to the provinces. This is the residual clause, and it fits in with the desire of the fathers of the federation to strengthen the hands of the Dominion Parliament by bestowing on it very extensive powers.

There is no doubt that this was originally intended to be the major source of Dominion power and the twenty-nine headings (see item (1) above) merely *examples* of the general grant. But the courts (for reasons which need not be elaborated) have taken the twenty-nine headings as embodying the chief powers of the Dominion, and have given to the provinces—through a generous interpretation of what can be placed under "property and civil rights"—the great bulk of the unallotted or unnamed residual powers. The courts decided, however, that the "peace, order, and good government" clause did give the Dominion a broad authority to act in time of grave national emergency, and that on such an occasion this power would override any of the powers of the provinces. The Dominion Parliament was thus able to fall back on this exceptional authority in both the World Wars; and it proceeded to fix prices, enact labour legislation, control rents, and exercise enormous powers in many fields without having to show any regard for provincial jurisdiction. As conditions returned to normal, however, the Dominion began to relinquish its emergency powers and retreated gradually to its usual and much more restricted field.

The consequences of the limitations imposed on the Dominion by this narrow interpretation of the residual or "peace, order, and good government" clause are these:

(*a*) The Dominion power, which the fathers of the Canadian federation had intended to be elastic and comprehensive, has become restricted and confined, while the provincial power has spread over most of the area thus left unoccupied. Residual power has in effect been shifted in the process of interpretation from the Dominion to the provinces. While this has been brought about by a series of judicial decisions, there is little doubt that the majority of the people were in favour of this change, for after 1867 there was a decided swing in favour of provincial rights. Today this swing in public opinion has to some degree been reversed, and there is a greater tendency to question the advisability of weakening the federal power.

(b) The great bulk of the more "modern" powers of government (which were of minor or no consequence in 1867 and were largely unmentioned) have thus gone to the provinces by virtue of the comprehensive covering clause of "property and civil rights". Jurisdiction over trade and marketing within the province, industrial disputes, trade-union legislation, workmen's compensation, hours of labour, wages, unemployment insurance,[1] and public health has been declared to be vested entirely or for the most part in the provincial legislatures. Legislation dealing with these matters cannot as a rule be passed on a national scale, but only by each province working within its own boundaries.

(c) Many of these new fields have proved to be expensive, and the provinces have often had difficulty in meeting additional demands on treasuries which were already hard pressed for funds. This question involves the financial side of the distribution of power and warrants separate discussion in the next chapter.

[1] This was transferred to the Dominion, however, by an amendment to the British North America Act in 1940.

CHAPTER FOUR

Dominion-Provincial Finance

THE founders of the Canadian federation considered that they were giving to the Dominion not only very substantial functions, but also those which were most likely to expand and to prove most expensive, notably national defence and the promotion of national development by great public works. They therefore gave the federal government unlimited powers of taxation. The provincial functions were to be much more modest and, it was thought, less likely to grow or to involve any very heavy financial burden. Three chief sources of revenue were accordingly to be available to the provinces: (1) direct taxes; (2) income of various kinds, including fees, licences, crown lands, royalties, etc.; (3) annual grants or subsidies paid by the Dominion on several grounds, the chief payment being one based on population. These were deemed sufficient to enable the provinces to carry on their activities in moderate comfort; indeed, for many years they had little need to make use of their power of direct taxation.

As time went on, however, provincial expenditure mounted and the early arrangements had to be substantially modified to produce adequate provincial revenues. One obvious method was for the Dominion to give larger subsidies, and on a number of occasions the provinces, both individually and collectively, were able to induce the Dominion to increase these annual payments.

The second method, of course, was for the provinces to use their power of imposing direct taxes; and taxes on income, estates of deceased persons, corporations, amusements, articles of consumption, and other items yielded a substantial return.

A new kind of Dominion payment, known as a grant-in-aid or conditional subsidy, was begun in 1912 and has been used to a varying degree ever since. This grant is made for a specified purpose on the condition that the province meet it with another and, as a rule, equal grant devoted to the same end and in accordance with standards laid down by the Dominion. Grants-in-aid have been paid to the provinces at one time or another for highways, old age pensions, technical and agricultural education, unemployment relief, public health, etc.

The result of all these expedients was to alleviate the provincial difficulties for a time; but as the expenditures continued to creep up, the provinces became increasingly aware of the very definite limitations in their capacity to carry the financial burden.

While it cannot be denied that some of the provincial distress was due to their own extravagance, a great part of their trouble was caused by factors over which they had little or no control. For one thing, their power to raise money by direct taxes was severely restricted by the ability—and willingness—of the Dominion to compete with them in the same taxing fields. The existence of income, inheritance, and sales taxes imposed by the Dominion inevitably meant that the potential provincial revenue from these sources was seriously impaired. Further, while the grant-in-aid device helped to give the provinces certain services which they badly needed, it did not as a rule help them to reduce expenditure. On the contrary, it often increased their outlay; for the provinces might be induced thereby to originate projects which they would otherwise have left alone and which some of them could ill afford, even in part, to maintain.

The most serious difficulty, however, was a fundamental lack of equilibrium between different aspects of the constitutional distribution of power, in that the number and expense of the provincial functions exceeded the funds which were available to pay for them. This was partly, but not entirely, due to the extension of provincial powers which had resulted from the interpretation of the residual or "peace, order, and good government" clause in the British North America Act. An equally important influence was a changing conception in the world as to what efforts a government can and should make to promote the welfare of its citizens; and it has so happened that legislation to meet these new needs has lain largely in the provincial field. Thus payments for unemployment, mothers' allowances, old age pensions, public health, etc., which were unknown in 1867, became provincial obligations, although the Dominion at times has given substantial assistance with a number of these payments. But even some of the old-established functions, such as highways and education, involved expenditures undreamt of seventy or eighty years ago. Thus in 1874 all the provinces of Canada spent only $4,000,000 on education and public welfare; but by 1937 this had multiplied over sixty times and had reached a total of $250,000,000!

A further disturbing factor has been the economic inequality of the provinces, so that these financial demands have not affected them all alike. The gap between the economically fortunate provinces and those which are not so well off is wide;[1] and financial arrangements which have enabled the wealthier provinces to meet their obligations have usually not been sufficient to relieve the stringency of those with more limited means. Provincial expenditure per capita on certain common and essential services, such as education, highways, public health, and public welfare, has varied greatly from province to province,[2] and the chief reason for

[1] Net production per capita in 1944 varied from $205.57 in Prince Edward Island to $681.92 in Ontario. In Prince Edward Island in 1937 the subsidy from the Dominion made up 41 per cent of the total revenue of the province; in New Brunswick, 20 per cent; in British Columbia, Quebec, and Ontario a trifling 5 per cent, 4.5 per cent, and 3 per cent respectively.
[2] In 1944-5 annual expenditure per pupil on education was as follows: Prince Edward Island $44.84, New Brunswick $66.26, Nova Scotia $73.93; while at the other extreme were Ontario $100.89; Manitoba $106.83, and British Columbia $120.01.

the difference has been the small per capita income of some provinces as compared to others. The Canadian nation is therefore not able to provide uniformity in the many services which are necessary to meet the primary needs of the citizen; for the extent and nature of those services has depended to an increasing degree upon the financial resources of the particular province in which a citizen happened to live.

An alarming financial situation in the nineteen-twenties became an intolerable one during the nineteen-thirties. The provinces were in no position to meet the additional strain which the depression placed on their resources; and this was greatly aggravated on the prairies by a succession of catastrophic crop failures. The depression demonstrated beyond any reasonable doubt that if the Canadian federation was to function effectively under modern conditions there would have to be a drastic revision of some of the constitutional arrangements between the Dominion and the provinces.

The Dominion government took action in 1937 by appointing a Royal Commission (the Rowell-Sirois Commission) to investigate Dominion-provincial relations with special attention to the financial problems involved. The report submitted by the Commission was focussed in the main on the two difficulties discussed above—the position of the provinces in relation to the federal government and the bearing which economic inequalities in the provinces had on matters of finance. The Commission suggested, for the first, a transfer of certain functions to the Dominion, accompanied by a relinquishment of provincial taxing powers;[1] and for the second, special annual payments by the Dominion to the more needy provinces which would enable them to maintain certain basic services at what was considered to be a minimum level for the entire Dominion. The report was considered at a Dominion-provincial conference; but it was not acceptable

---

[1]More specifically, the Dominion was to assume provincial (but not municipal) debt and take over a few provincial functions, especially the responsibility for unemployment relief. The provinces were to relinquish all right to impose income, corporation, and inheritance taxes.

to some provinces, and further consideration was postponed until after the war.

The pressing demands of the war forced the Dominion to assume a large measure of control over many taxes, and it paid the provincial governments (as a temporary measure) substantial annual amounts in exchange for a free hand in several important fields of taxation, notably personal and corporation income taxes. The war left three firm imprints in Dominion-provincial finance which have materially affected subsequent policy: (1) the desire of the Dominion to retain many of the exclusive financial powers which it had exercised during the war and which seemed increasingly necessary in view of the burden of public debt, the high costs of reconstruction, the need of avoiding conflicting federal and provincial policies, etc.; (2) the apparent feasibility of paying large Dominion subsidies to the provinces in exchange for the provincial relinquishment of their major taxes; (3) the conviction that national financial policies alone were competent to cope with emergency conditions on a large scale, and that the economic life of the nation could be moulded to an appreciable degree by vigorous financial measures.

At the conclusion of the war the Dominion therefore brought before another conference new proposals based on its war experience. These proposals included an extensive programme of social security and welfare measures to be undertaken by the Dominion, and greatly increased subsidies (based largely on population) to be paid to the provinces provided they would remain out of the income tax, corporation tax, and inheritance tax fields. Once again, however, all the provinces were unwilling to accept them, especially Ontario and Quebec, who considered that they would lose far more than they would gain under the new plan. Unable to secure unanimity, the Dominion in 1946 repeated substantially the same offer to the provinces individually, and within a year all except Ontario and Quebec had made separate agreements with the federal government for a five-year experimental period. The terms of union with Newfoundland contemplated a possible agreement similar to those made with the seven provinces, but any such arrangement was to await the action of the new provincial government.

The existing agreements need not be given in detail, for they vary somewhat, and the provinces were offered alternative schemes for calculating the annual subsidy. The subsidy under all the schemes is a substantial one, and varies from $17 per capita (as offered to Quebec) to $24 for Prince Edward Island, on 1947 figures.[1] The provinces entering into the agreement have in return relinquished income, corporation, and inheritance taxes. The original proposals of 1945-6 contemplated that the Dominion would also initiate a programme for the development of natural resources, would be responsible for projects of public works to relieve unemployment, would launch a public health insurance scheme, and would assume complete or partial responsibility for different groups of unemployed; but these and other measures were deferred until all the provinces became parties to the agreement. In May, 1948, however, the Dominion submitted to Parliament a public health assistance programme which was designed to prepare the way for a more ambitious scheme in this field.

In short, while very sweeping changes have recently taken place in Dominion-provincial finance, the relations have not yet become stabilized. A firm settlement will probably have to wait until Ontario and Quebec are prepared to agree to the existing proposals or until the Dominion produces an entirely new plan which will be acceptable to all ten provinces.

[1] A minimum payment is guaranteed, and this may be augmented with increases in national population and national income. The amounts given above for 1947 are slightly more than the minimum.

CHAPTER FIVE

The Governor-General

THE executive government and authority of Canada is vested in the King, who delegates his authority (on the advice of his Canadian Cabinet) to his representative, the Governor-General. The Governor-General, however, exercises in reality very few powers in his own right as a person. His principal function is to represent the Crown, the institution which embodies the executive authority; and in this capacity he rarely takes the initiative himself or follows his own inclinations, but rather speaks and acts in accordance with the counsel given him by his constitutional advisers, the Cabinet. This is, of course, simply another example of the Canadian practice following that in England, where long ago this singular but highly successful method was adopted as a means of bringing an autocratic monarch under the control of the representatives of the people.

Governors, like Kings, have not always been so powerless. The early Governors in Canada exercised genuine authority: they directed the operation of the government in the colony (as noted in Chapter I), and they also acted as the local representative of the British government. The establishment of a responsible Cabinet involved the transfer of the greater part of the Governor's power in local affairs to his Cabinet, and the extent of that transfer steadily increased until the Governor-General today occupies substantially the same position in relation to his government as does the King in relation to the government in Great Britain. The Governor-General's activity as the representative or agent of the British government also rapidly declined as Canada asserted its growing independence, and this function completely vanished after the Imperial Conference of 1926. The Governor-General is now appointed by the King on the advice of the Canadian Cabinet, and he has no connexion whatever with the government of Great Britain. He holds office at the pleasure of the Canadian government and the term is normally a period of five years.

In most formal matters the Cabinet acts through the Governor-General and in the name of the Governor-General-in-Council, which is simply the Governor speaking under the advice of the Cabinet. But in matters of an international character, the declaration of war, the appointment of ambassadors, the ratification of treaties, etc., the Cabinet acts not through the Governor but through the King. The much greater convenience of giving advice directly to the Governor-General will probably lead in the future to a gradual abandonment of the practice of using the King in such matters, and there is no legal barrier to prevent this short-cut being adopted at any time.

While the aggressive vitality of the Governor-General has disappeared from Canadian government, he has still valuable duties to perform. He takes from the shoulders of the Prime Minister many tiresome routine tasks of a social and ceremonial nature; he is sometimes useful in general diplomatic relations with the United States; and he may be able to furnish the Cabinet with unbiased and helpful advice on matters of state. One of the most important of his functions is to select a new Prime Minister whenever the office becomes vacant. On most occasions, the vacancy will occur as a result of the defeat of a Government,[1] and the finding of a successor will then be nothing more than routine, for the Governor-General will simply send for the Leader of the Opposition. If the office is vacant because the majority party has lost its leader, there will be no question of the

[1] The word "Government" (with a capital letter) is used here and hereafter as an alternative term for "Cabinet".

successor if the party has had time to make its own selection. Thus in 1948 the Governor-General asked Mr. L. S. St. Laurent, the newly elected leader of the Liberal party, to become Prime Minister in place of Mr. Mackenzie King, who had resigned. But vacancies cannot always be anticipated, and there will be occasions when there may be genuine uncertainty as to who should become Prime Minister. At such a juncture it is highly desirable to have someone charged with the duty of inviting a suitable person to form a Government, subject, of course, to that person being able to obtain the support of the House of Commons. Cabinet government, in fact, presupposes the existence of someone who is in a position to issue such an invitation. In Great Britain this function has always been discharged by the King, and in the Dominions, by the Governor-General.

In addition to the above contingency in which the Governor is expected to take personal initiative, there may be certain very rare occasions when he may feel obliged to intervene in the normal routine of government, reject the advice of his Cabinet, and act on his own responsibility. The exceptional nature of this step, however, cannot be too heavily emphasized. His normal function is to follow the advice given him by his Cabinet even though he may believe that advice to be foolish or wrong. The Cabinet is in charge of the government; it is responsible to Parliament; and it is accordingly bound to defend the decisions of the Governor as its own, which, in reality, they are. Yet long constitutional usage also recognizes that under certain circumstances the Governor-General possesses a reserve power of interference, although the occasions for its exercise may not occur once in a generation. While the nature of these occasions cannot be defined with any exactness, it may be said that the Governor, broadly speaking, will be justified in acting to protect the normal working of the constitution when the usual procedures prove insufficient or inadequate. Thus, if a Prime Minister were to accept a bribe and were to refuse either to resign or to advise the Governor to summon Parliament to deal with the matter, the Governor-General could with perfect constitutional propriety dismiss him from office. Or if a Prime Minister who had obtained a dissolution of Parliament and was returned with a minority of members in the House of Commons immediately advised another dissolution, the Governor-General could refuse the advice and thus force the resignation of the Cabinet. Incidents of this kind will happily be very rare; but in a constitution which depends in large measure upon the proper observance of custom rather than law, an emergency insurance against a possible abuse of some of these understandings is not without value. The mere existence of such a power and the knowledge that it can be invoked will almost certainly suffice to prevent the occasion for its exercise arising at all.

It is evident that if the best use is to be made of the Governor-General, he should be strictly neutral in Canadian politics even as the King is above the prejudices and antagonisms of politics in Great Britain. The value of the office in both countries depends entirely upon the willingness of the incumbent to forego his own wishes and opinions, to devote himself with a single mind to the public good, and to be content with exercising a moderating influence quietly and without public acknowledgment and acclaim. A Governor who is not politically impartial or who is even suspected of partiality will not only prove useless, he will seriously imperil the working of constitutional government itself. This indispensable prerequisite is the justification for recruiting Governors-General from outside Canada. Few, if any, Canadians of sufficient prominence could be found whose past careers would not disclose some affiliation or sympathy with a Canadian political party which might prove embarrassing to a Governor. They need not, of course, be chosen always from Great Britain; and it is possible that the Dominions might conveniently draw on one another's resources when making appointments to this position.

CHAPTER SIX

The Cabinet

THE Cabinet has been described as "the mainspring of government", a phrase that indicates the central and indispensable position which it occupies among all the government agencies. The King, or his deputy, the Governor-General, is the nominal executive and head of the state; but the Prime Minister and the Cabinet form the active executive which drives the entire mechanism. The Cabinet formulates and supervises the carrying out of all executive policies. Its members oversee the administration of all government departments. It directs the preparation of all important legislation, and it guides the passage of that legislation through Parliament. It also exercises important legislative powers of its own.

The Cabinet is not expressly recognized anywhere in the British North America Act and (as mentioned in an earlier chapter) it is almost completely ignored in the statute book. It exists outside the law, though not, of course, contrary to it. The Cabinet's informal activities as a planning body and as the directing agency of the party in office are not the concern of the law, while the Cabinet's formal activities are not conducted under its own name but under that of the legally constituted Privy Council. Once again the wording of the constitution is seen to be at variance with the actual facts. The Privy Council of Canada is made up of those who are appointed by the Governor-General, and it includes all members of past and present Cabinets as well as a number of other distinguished persons from Canada and elsewhere. The complete membership of this motley body, however, does nothing, and it has met only once in its entire history.[1] The active part of it, the Cabinet which is in office for the moment, meets frequently, and this segment, acting on behalf of and in the name of the whole, formally advises the Governor-General to give his consent to various measures, which then emerge as minutes or orders-in-council passed by the "Governor-General-in-Council".

CABINET PERSONNEL

The Prime Minister is the head of the Cabinet and far surpasses his colleagues in importance and power. He takes office at the instance of the Governor-General who requests him to form a Cabinet or Government. The right of these members to hold office thus depends on their being invited by the Prime Minister to attend Cabinet meetings. If they are not already Privy Councillors, they will first be sworn in as members of that body. The great majority of the Cabinet members are also heads of the executive departments of government—the Minister of Finance, the Secretary of State for External Affairs, the Minister of Justice, etc. The Cabinet may also include one or more members who have no departments to supervise (known as Ministers without portfolio), and recent custom ensures that the Government Leader in the Senate will be in this category.

There have, however, been rare cases where a person was head of a department and one of the ministerial group, but was not admitted to Cabinet membership. Some mention should also be made of a number of parliamentary assistants, who are attached to various Ministers yet are not considered to be in either Cabinet or Ministry, although they go out of office when the Cabinet retires.

All the above persons—whether members of the Cabinet or not—must by invariable custom have seats in Parliament which, in almost every instance, means seats in the House of

[1] The one meeting was on July 31, 1947, and was summoned to receive a message from the King announcing his formal consent to the engagement of Princess Elizabeth.

Commons. The Government Leader in the Senate is clearly not a member of the House, and there have been one or two minor exceptions since this customary rule of a seat in the Commons was begun in 1921. While the Prime Minister will normally select his Cabinet from members in Parliament, he will at times go to a provincial legislature or elsewhere for fresh material; and these new members must, of course, find seats in the House within a reasonable time.

Although the number of Cabinet members and their selection depend on the wishes of the Prime Minister, his choice is influenced by many considerations. Each province considers that it is entitled to its own representative in the Cabinet, and the large provinces not unnaturally demand more than one representative. If Quebec is given an English-speaking member (which is customary), it must also have at least three or four French-speaking members, and this almost automatically raises the Ontario quota to four and probably five. The Cabinet thus becomes in large measure a federal body. It is usual, indeed, to recognize that each member speaks with special authority when any matter involving his province arises for settlement, although the particular subject may have nothing whatever to do with the department of which that member is the head.

But the Prime Minister does not stop at giving special representation to the provinces; he must also recognize a host of other interests. The Acadian French, the Irish Roman Catholics, the trade unions, the farmers, the financial interests, the Orange Order, and others will all urge their claims, and some of them at least will be recognized. A further complication is that certain portfolios are apt to become identified with certain areas—Agriculture with the prairies; Fisheries with British Columbia and the Maritime Provinces; Finance with Eastern Canada—and these affiliations are rarely disregarded. Although one member may be able to fill several requirements, the need to meet many of these demands inevitably tends to enlarge the Cabinet unduly.

Sixteen or seventeen is the usual number of members, but it may even reach twenty or twenty-one. The efforts of the Prime Minister to keep the number of members within reasonable limits have been aided in recent years by the creation of parliamentary assistants. These have, as it were, one foot in the Council chamber, and their careful selection may be of material assistance in meeting the demands for sectional representation.

THE POSITION OF THE CABINET

The fundamental constitutional principle concerning the Cabinet has already been noted: it is responsible to the House of Commons and must at all times enjoy its support. Failing this, it must either resign or dissolve the House in the hope that it will be able to obtain the necessary support in the new House after the election. The responsibility to the Commons is both individual and collective. Each Minister is responsible for the work of his special department, and all are as a group responsible for one another's individual acts as well as for Government policy as a whole. This produces the "solidarity" of the Cabinet: all must agree in public on all matters of major policy, and they thereby become in effect responsible to one another. Unity is maintained the more easily by another Cabinet practice, its secrecy. All members are by virtue of their Privy Council oath bound to keep secret all Cabinet proceedings, with the result that any Cabinet disagreements in private are not easily discovered by the Opposition parties, who would naturally turn them to excellent advantage in the House and elsewhere.

The Cabinet is able to rely on a consistent vote in the House of Commons largely because of the party system. The supporters of the Cabinet have been elected as members of a common political party and as followers of the party leader, and they thus tend to give constant endorsement to the measures which the Government introduces and sponsors.

A vote against the party would also be contrary to the traditions and habits of a lifetime, and to oppose their own colleagues and the party organization would be regarded by most members as little short of treachery.

The reliability of the party member is enhanced by party practices and inducements designed for the purpose. Each party in Parliament, for example, holds at intervals private meetings or caucuses to which all its members are invited for the purpose of discussing various proposals and of determining the party stand on these and other questions. Frank criticism from all members is expected, although it is understood that members (except in most unusual circumstances) will accept the decision of the caucus as binding on them in any proceedings in the House. Patronage is another factor in maintaining discipline in the ranks of the majority party. It may take the form of minor jobs in the civil service for party workers in whom a member is interested, or of a coveted promotion or position for the member himself. Either form is likely to have the same soothing effect and induce the member to look more sympathetically on the measures which the party wishes to have adopted.

The power of the Prime Minister over his Cabinet is potentially enormous, although the degree and manner in which it is used will depend in large measure on the leader himself. He not only appoints the Ministers to the Cabinet, but he may also demand their resignations any time he sees fit. He presides over Cabinet meetings, and his wishes will invariably receive special consideration and usually unhesitating support. Yet his firmness must always be tempered with tact and shrewdness. For the Ministers are his colleagues and not his subordinates, and a rebellious Cabinet can usually hold its own against any Prime Minister, as, indeed, one did in the Bowell Cabinet crisis in 1896. The Prime Minister must know when to command, when to persuade, and when to give way. He can never be really independent of his Cabinet any more than he or his colleagues can ever be really independent of the House of Commons. His leadership in both bodies is expected and demanded, and general acquiescence can within limits be assumed; but this co-operation is usually given with some reserve, and the possibility of dissatisfaction and even revolt, though it may be remote, is never entirely absent. An able Prime Minister will thus appear to get his way in the Cabinet or in the House, but in some instances at least this success will spring from the fact that he has been sufficiently wise and far-seeing to limit his demands and to confine his proposals to those which will gain the general acceptance of his followers. Support, and even cheerful support, in the House is essential, and no Prime Minister is so powerful that he can afford to neglect either the votes themselves or the feelings and emotions which lie behind the votes.

The Cabinet discharges both executive and legislative functions: the first, in the Council chamber and in the separate departments; the second, chiefly in the House of Commons.

EXECUTIVE FUNCTIONS

The Cabinet must take the lead in the initiation and development of national policies, both in domestic and in foreign affairs. In this task it receives incalculable assistance from the civil servants, who not only supply the solid bed of information on which these policies must be built, but also furnish the framework of many of the policies themselves. It may also avail itself of other sources of information—the views of economic and social groups which are likely to be affected by its proposals, of party organizations, of a select committee appointed by the House of Commons, or of a Royal Commission of inquiry created on the initiative of the Cabinet itself.

Each individual Minister is particularly charged with the duty of directing the work of his own department. He oversees its administration; he speaks in the House on its behalf;

he answers questions there concerning its many activities; he ensures that Parliament passes the necessary appropriations to pay for its undertakings. He places the aims, endeavours, and achievements of his department before the general public, and he also discharges the reverse function of seeing that his departmental officials are made aware of the interests of the public and are not forgetful of the primary ends the department is designed to accomplish.

The Cabinet is the only body on which all departments are represented, and it is therefore peculiarly adapted to the work of co-ordinating government policies at the highest level. This function is not, however, as a rule, very well performed, for the pressure of other business is so great that the Cabinet has little time to consider any but the most urgent and inescapable problems of this kind.

Finally, the Cabinet is especially responsible for the performance of a number of specific executive acts, usually in the name of the Governor-General (or the King) and on the immediate initiative of the Prime Minister. It thus makes all important appointments, removes public officials, pardons offenders, ratifies treaties and takes other formal action in international affairs. It summons, prorogues, and dissolves Parliament.[1] It also deals with a number of matters relating to the provinces. It disallows provincial acts; it makes decisions on provincial bills which have been reserved for its consideration;[2] it hears appeals from sectarian minorities on educational matters and takes appropriate action.[3]

LEGISLATIVE FUNCTIONS

The Cabinet's power over the House of Commons lies at the root of its responsibility for all major legislation. The power is derived, of course, from its command over the party

---

[1] The summoning of Parliament is simply calling it into session when necessary. Prorogation is the act of terminating a parliamentary session. Dissolution brings the life of a Parliament to an end, and hence must be followed by a general election.
[2] See p. 104.
[3] See p. 27.

majority; while its command over the majority comes from those party influences which have been already noted, reinforced by the prestige and ability of the Prime Minister, the general capacity of the Cabinet, and the majority's fear of doing anything which would assist the Opposition in discrediting the Government. Should its support show signs of flagging, the Cabinet will not hesitate to call for a vote in the House and compel the waverers to face the alternative of sustaining the Government or encompassing its defeat. The party majority also places in the Cabinet's hands the determination of the daily order of business of the House, and allows it within limits to pre-empt the time which is necessary for the discussion of the measures which it wishes to have enacted. However, conviction and enlightened self-interest can be relied upon to restrain a Cabinet from any marked abuse of a power which is likely to prove ephemeral.[1]

A short digression is necessary here in order to explain the different kinds of bills which are considered by Parliament and which, in due course, may become acts of Parliament or statutes. They may be classified as follows:

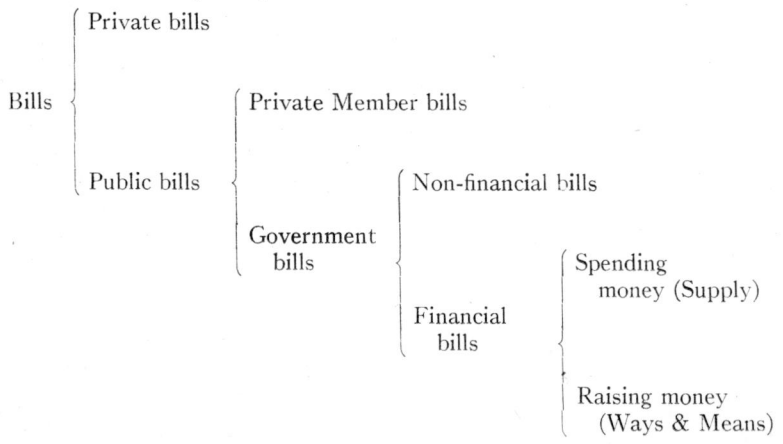

Bills
- Private bills
- Public bills
  - Private Member bills
  - Government bills
    - Non-financial bills
    - Financial bills
      - Spending money (Supply)
      - Raising money (Ways & Means)

Private bills are comparatively unimportant and affect primarily individuals, corporations, or special localities. Bills

[1] See pp. 88-90.

to incorporate a company or to divorce married persons are examples.

Public bills deal with matters of a public or general nature and form by far the major part of all bills considered by the House of Commons. They fall into two chief classes. If introduced by a member of the Ministry or a parliamentary assistant, they are known as *Government bills.* If they are introduced by a private member (whether from the Government or Opposition side) they are called *Private Member bills.*

Government bills again may be sub-divided into *bills dealing with finance* and other or *non-financial bills.* These terms are self-explanatory, although the actual line of demarkation is not always easy to draw.

Finally, financial bills may be concerned with spending money, the chief of which are known as *supply bills;* or with raising money, when they may be referred to as *ways and means* or *taxing bills.*

The Cabinet dominates the consideration and passage of bills of all kinds. However, it rarely chooses to take any stand on private bills, which are not at all likely to affect Government policy. Similarly private member bills are usually of little concern to the Cabinet; they are naturally under the especial care of the members who have introduced them. They rarely make much progress in the House because of the limited time and opportunity available for their consideration.

Government bills are an entirely different matter. These, it is obvious, must be the chief interest of the Cabinet and therefore of the House. They constitute the Cabinet's legislative programme, and the Cabinet sees that they receive whatever time, attention, and support may be necessary to ensure their passage. So convinced, indeed, is the Cabinet of the importance and merit of these measures that it will insist that their acceptance by the House is essential to its continuance in office. The application of this maxim of "Love me, love my dog" therefore means that a vote against a Government bill is a vote against the Government, and a defeat of a Government bill will force either the Cabinet's resignation or a general election.

The Cabinet has a particular responsibility—imposed on it by both constitutional law and custom—for Government bills which deal with finance. No bill to spend money or to impose a tax can even be considered by the House except on the initiative of the Cabinet, nor can anyone but a Minister move in the House to have an expenditure or a tax increased. Any member, however, may move for a reduction. These special powers of initiation and amendment, joined to the Cabinet's normal command over the House, give it complete control in all matters of finance. The body which initiates all expenditures of government is the same body which must devise the means for raising the funds with which to pay its bills. The power is admittedly enormous, but it finds its great justification in the increased concentration of responsibility and the resulting incentives to economy.

The Cabinet also exercises a *direct* legislative authority by its ability (acting as the Governor-in-Council) to enact orders-in-council. The great bulk of these, however, are not legislative in character, but deal with executive functions, appointments, contracts, etc. (Thus during the Second World War not more than 5 per cent of such orders were considered to be legislative measures.) This subsidiary legislative authority is delegated to the Cabinet by many acts of Parliament, and its powers are, of course, limited by the terms of the delegation. The great merit of orders-in-council (which will number thousands a year) is the comparative ease of their passage and the resulting flexibility which they give to a statute and to other orders passed under its provisions. An excessive use of orders-in-council constitutes a serious disregard of the position and value of Parliament: their moderate use is on the whole beneficial and forms a necessary aid to the work of modern governments.

CHAPTER SEVEN

The Civil Service and the Departments

THE Cabinet Ministers are in charge of and responsible for the enforcement and the administration of the laws, but the vast bulk of the work is done by the paid officials of the Government, the civil servants, who hold permanent positions and therefore do not go out of office with the Cabinet. The civil servants range all the way from elevator attendants and farm hands to the deputy minister, who is the top official in each department and who works directly under the Minister himself. Between these extremes is represented almost every occupation in Canada. In 1948 there were about 118,000 persons in the employ of the federal government. This does not include Dominion employees in such organizations as the Canadian National Railways, the Canadian Broadcasting Corporation, and the Bank of Canada.

The duties of the civil servants are to carry out the law and to enforce the department's policies. Those in the higher ranks are expected also to produce helpful suggestions derived in large measure from the problems encountered in the actual work of administration, and thus to provide the Minister with the ideas and facts on which departmental policies are formed. But though the civil servant gives information and advice to the political head, the Minister, it is the latter who must assume the responsibility of making final decisions.

A Minister is rarely a technical expert in the special field in which his department operates, and he will therefore not have the preconceived ideas and the narrow outlook which a specialized training is likely to produce. A political non-technical Minister is more likely to come to departmental problems with a fresh mind, an impatience with red tape and outworn procedures, a willingness to consider the needs of his department in association with his colleagues who have similar and often competing demands in their departments. These characteristics thus tend to make his influence in the department both stimulating and beneficial.

The Minister is, of course, perfectly free to go against the advice which is tendered him by his civil servants. In such an event, it then becomes the duty of the civil servants to devote their best endeavours to the task of making the Minister's policy work, even though they may in the first instance have advised against it. The key to the situation lies in the political responsibility of the Minister for all the policies and activities of the department of which he is the head. He takes the blame when things go wrong; he takes what little credit he can when things turn out well. It is obvious that under the circumstances no one but the Minister can exercise the power of final decision in the department, for power and political responsibility are inseparably linked together.

APPOINTMENT AND TENURE

Forty or fifty years ago civil servants were appointed at the instance of members of Parliament and those defeated candidates who belonged to the majority party in the Commons. A fairly large number of the minor posts are still filled in that way. But the greater part of the expert, high-grade, and medium personnel and many in the lower grades of the service are now appointed only after their ability has been demonstrated by some objective competitive tests, such as written and oral examinations, practical work, letters of recommendation, and past record. The tests are given by examiners under the Civil Service Commission, an impartial body which is appointed for the purpose.

This non-partisan system of appointment by merit began in 1908 and was applied generally throughout the service in 1918. It represents a great advance on the patronage system. It usually attracts and secures better men; it is more likely to place the right man in the most suitable position; it cultivates in the civil servant a healthier attitude to his work and improves relations with the Minister and fellow employees.

The tenure enjoyed in the service has, broadly speaking, changed with the change in the method of appointment. Originally the civil servants were expected to be active in support of the political party which had appointed them; and if their party failed to win the election, the unhappy workers often found themselves thrown out of employment. Such dismissals are now rare. The tradition of an impartial non-political service has become firmly established during the past thirty years, and the quality and status of its personnel have been enormously improved thereby. Public officials today pride themselves on their objectivity and their ability to serve with equal zeal any party which gains power. A change of Minister or Cabinet affects the attitude of a civil servant little more than a new general manager or board of directors affects the attitude of an employee in a private business.

ADMINISTRATIVE POWERS

The tendency of modern government is inevitably to expand the civil service, to raise the standards of its membership, and to place more and more reliance on its judgment in matters of administration. All these developments spring in large measure from the greatly increased functions of government and the highly complex nature of much of the work of administration today. The idea of a century ago that the chief business of the state was to give protection against foreign enemies, to maintain law and order, and to conduct a few public enterprises has completely vanished. A modern government is expected to guard public health, to take care of the sick and aged, to set rates and charges for many semi-public services, to supervise financial enterprises, to conduct research, to regulate industry, hours of labour, wages, sanitation, etc., and even to own and operate great industrial undertakings.[1] These many and varied activities of government obviously demand a large and highly skilled civil service.

But they do more. They not only thrust an extremely heavy burden on the administration, they compel the administration to assume a load of a new kind. In former times the civil servant was given a law to enforce; and that law in the main was negative in its effect. It stated what the individual should not do, and punished anyone who stepped over these limits. Many of the laws today are still in the form of prohibitions, although these have tended to be much more complex than formerly. Others place positive obligations on the citizen. This in turn will often compel the government official to set standards or to define goals which must be reached, and then to demand certain action from the citizen and to decide whether the action which is forthcoming is sufficient to comply with the requirements of the law.

All these detailed provisions cannot be enumerated by Parliament nor can their application and enforcement be supervised by the courts. Parliament does not have the specialized knowledge, nor could it make its legislation flexible enough to cover all the wide variety of contingencies which might arise. Similarly the courts cannot be expected to intervene effectively to protect the citizen from every possible abuse of administrative power. To saddle the courts with such a task would be to impose on them an intolerable burden of hundreds of thousands of new cases; and it would demand of them a highly specialized knowledge and a broad sympathy in the application of that knowledge which, in the

[1]See pp. 13, 33.

nature of things, the courts can scarcely be expected to possess. In many cases, moreover, the aggrieved or interested parties can ill afford the heavy expense and long delays which are the almost inescapable consequences of court procedure.

The administrative arm of government (subject, of course, to the control of the Cabinet) is thus given the statutory power of passing rules and regulations for the better realization of the purposes of Parliament. These orders have all the force of law and are rarely made to depend on later parliamentary approval. A body of civil servants (or the Minister) may also be given the right to hear appeals by dissatisfied persons from rulings or judgments given by other civil servants in cases under dispute, and the aggrieved party may even be forbidden to appeal the decision to the courts of law. It is evident that under these conditions the rule of law[1]—and with it the rights of the citizen—is substantially weakened. Discretionary powers are thereby greatly increased; and inasmuch as the courts are not allowed to review all cases, they are unable to give the citizen the final protection from abuses which may conceivably develop in the course of administration.

While it is true, as suggested above, that many delegations of power may be inescapable, it is none the less necessary to take precautionary measures which will help to restrict the number of such delegations and confine their use so far as may be consistent with the attainment of reasonable administrative efficiency. This can be achieved to a material degree by more careful legislation. Parliament can ensure that the statutes define the discretionary areas with precision and that these areas be kept as narrow as efficient administration will allow. Parliament can also hold the Cabinet to a strict accountability for the exercise of all administrative discretionary power and can keep all such actions under its diligent scrutiny. The chief guardian against abuses is

[1] See pp. 12-13.

therefore an alert and even suspicious Parliament, which is encouraged and supported by a public opinion fully alive to the dangerous possibilities which are always latent in modern administrative procedures.

THE DEPARTMENTS

The task of administration is apportioned among a number of departments chiefly on the basis of the nature of the work performed. Each of these, as already noted, is directed by a Cabinet Minister, assisted by a deputy minister as the permanent head of the civil servants in that department. Under the deputy are the heads of the main branches of that department's activity. Each of these in turn supervises the heads of the different divisions, and the work and oversight are progressively divided and delegated until the most humble member is reached at the base of the departmental pyramid. Each official is thus made responsible to the one above him, he to the next in line, and so on, until the pyramid of responsibility reaches its apex with the deputy and the Minister.

The departments (in alphabetical order) and some of their activities are as follows:

1. *Agriculture.* Inasmuch as agriculture is a field of concurrent jurisdiction with the provinces, the work of this department is closely associated with that of the Departments of Agriculture under the provincial governments. The federal department conducts many scientific services, undertakes economic research, maintains experimental farms and stations across the Dominion, and gives leadership and information to various activities associated with agricultural production and marketing.

2. *External Affairs.* This has charge of Canada's relations within the Commonwealth, with foreign countries, and with the United Nations. In 1948 Canada was represented abroad by High Commissioners in six other parts of the Commonwealth, and by ambassadors or other diplomatic or consular

SUPREME COURT OF CANADA BUILDING, OTTAWA

National Film Board

OPENING OF GRAND JURY SESSIONS, TORONTO

By Special Permission of the Court

LEGISLATIVE BUILDINGS, VICTORIA

B.C. Government Travel Bureau

LEGISLATIVE ASSEMBLY CHAMBER, FREDERICTON

New Brunswick Government

agents in some twenty foreign capitals. In one year Canada has sent representatives to as many as ninety-five international conferences, and she is a constant and active participant in a wide variety of international organizations.

3. *Finance.* This is the most important of all the departments, and its activities extend throughout the whole service. It supervises, controls, and directs the great bulk of matters relating to the public accounts, revenues, and expenditures of Canada. It gathers together and checks the estimated expenditures for all departments and presents them to the Treasury Board[1] and the Council for their approval. It prepares the estimated revenues and the financial proposals which are later submitted in the budget by the Minister of Finance. One of its officials, the Comptroller of the Treasury, supervises and controls the payment of all moneys from the Consolidated Revenue Fund, which is the gigantic pool into which all the revenues of the government are paid. The Royal Canadian Mint, the Bank of Canada, the Foreign Exchange Control Board, the Tariff Board, and other bodies are to a varying degree under the Minister of Finance.

4. *Fisheries.* It renders protection to both sea and inland fisheries, and conducts investigation and research on many problems connected with the industry. Widely different fishing conditions in different provinces and special arrangements which have been made with some provinces and not with others, have resulted in a pronounced lack of uniformity in Dominion participation in this activity.

5. *Justice.* It has charge of all matters connected with the administration of justice which are not under provincial jurisdiction, and it advises all federal departments on legal questions. It superintends the penitentiaries and the Mounted Police.

6. *Labour.* Labour problems are, broadly speaking, under provincial jurisdiction; but the Dominion has authority over those arising in transport and communication agencies which

[1]See p. 82*n*.

extend beyond provincial boundaries and in works declared by Parliament to be for the general advantage of Canada. Seamen, however, come under the Canada Shipping Act, which is the concern of the Department of Transport. The facilities of the Department of Labour are available, if needed by the provinces, and it co-operates with them on many matters. A Dominion grant-in-aid for vocational training and apprenticeship is administered by this department. It also collects a great deal of statistical material on labour questions and makes this available through numerous publications. The administration of the Unemployment Insurance Act is entrusted to a Commission under the Minister of Labour.

7. *Mines and Resources.* This is an omnibus department, and the names of the chief branches—Lands, Parks, and Forests, Mines and Geology, Surveys and Engineering, Indian Affairs, and Immigration—will give some idea of the diversity of its work. In a number of these fields the department works in close association with the provincial governments which carry on related activities. It has charge also of the Yukon and North-West Territories.

8. *National Defence.* This department has the responsibility for the three armed services, Navy, Army, and Air Force, as well as the special branch of Defence Research.

9. *National Health and Welfare.* It has charge of general questions concerning national health, pure food regulations, control of narcotics, and of certain specialized health activities, the chief responsibility for which rests with the provinces. It administers the family allowances, the old age pensions (with the provinces), and the physical fitness programme (another grant-in-aid scheme with the provinces).

10. *National Revenue.* This is a collecting agency for the federal government and its work involves the collection of customs duties, personal and corporation income taxes, excise taxes, excess profits taxes, succession (or inheritance) duties, and miscellaneous taxes.

11. *Post Office*. This is simply a gigantic business run by the federal government, which provides postal and allied services.

12. *Public Works*. The department is a "servicing" agency for other departments of government, and as such has charge of all Dominion public buildings. It also constructs and maintains wharves, breakwaters, and general harbour facilities, though not those which have been placed under the National Harbours Board.

13. *Reconstruction and Supply*. The war brought part of this department into existence, and its functions have been gradually adjusted to deal with what are primarily post-war problems, such as housing, industrial development, community planning, research, and conservation of natural resources.

14. *Secretary of State*. This is a clearing-house for communications with the Lieutenant-Governors and provincial governments. It is also another omnibus department. It deals with matters arising under the Dominion Companies Act, the Canadian Citizenship Act, the Copyright Act, and the Patents Act. It has charge of the Department of Public Printing and the Public Archives.

15. *Trade and Commerce*. It provides information and assistance to Canadian firms interested in foreign trade or to foreigners interested in Canadian trade, and it maintains a trade commissioner service in many countries. It participates in international fairs; endeavours to encourage tourists to come to Canada; and administers steamship subsidies. It also provides for the inspection of weights and measures and other standards. The Dominion Bureau of Statistics, which compiles and publishes statistical material on a wide variety of subjects, is attached to this department.

16. *Transport*. This department has the oversight and regulation of civil aviation and radio communication, and provides meteorological services throughout Canada. It also has charge of navigation aids of all kinds, such as lighthouses

and buoys; the supervision of shipping registry; the certification of navigation officers; and the maintenance of icebreakers, ice patrol services, etc. The National Harbours Board, the Board of Transport Commissioners, and Trans-Canada Air Lines report to Parliament through the Minister of Transport.

17. *Veterans Affairs.* This is responsible for the medical treatment, hospitalization, training, and re-establishment into civil life of all veterans. Pensions, however, are entrusted to the Pension Commission, an independent body, which co-operates with the department, but is not under it.

BOARDS AND COMMISSIONS

In addition to these regular services there are a number of boards and commissions which do not fit into the departmental scheme. Each is constituted under a separate statute. They differ widely in function; their members hold office for different terms and under different tenure; and they exercise a varying degree of independence of the Cabinet, which turns for the most part upon the nature of the work they perform. Despite this variety, they can be classified roughly into three chief groups:

1. Those whose functions are largely *advisory.* The Historic Sites and Monuments Board, for example, is a body of prominent historians who meet once a year to advise the National Parks Bureau on the restoration, preservation, and marking of historic buildings and sites throughout Canada.

2. Those which are concerned with *regulation, supervision.* or *administration* or any combination of these functions. The Pension Commission thus administers the Pension Act and awards pensions to war veterans; the Civil Service Commission administers the Civil Service Act, examines candidates for entrance to the service, directs its organization, and oversees promotions. The Board of Grain Commissioners applies the terms of the Grain Act to the operations of the grain trade. The Board of Transport Commissioners

hears disputes, fixes rates, investigates accidents, and performs many other duties connected with the railways as well as having jurisdiction over the operations of express companies, telephones, telegraphs, aeroplanes, and inland water carriers.

3. Those which are primarily *operating* bodies and are engaged on work of essentially the same character as a private business. In this class fall the Bank of Canada, the Canadian National Railways, the Canadian Broadcasting Corporation, the National Harbours Board, Trans-Canada Air Lines, etc. Each of these is operated by an executive board which bears a close resemblance to a board of directors of a private company. The Dominion Government exercises at best a very indirect control over the activities of these enterprises, and the general aim is to place them in a position where they can operate under substantially the same conditions as surround similar organizations in the business world.

CHAPTER EIGHT

The Senate

THE Parliament of Canada is made up of the King (represented by the Governor-General), the Senate, and the House of Commons, and the consent of all three is necessary for the passage of legislation. The consent of the Governor in this respect can always be assumed, for here he invariably acts on the advice of his Cabinet, and the Cabinet must favour the bill or it would never have allowed it to pass the Commons. The consent of the Senate, however, cannot be taken for granted. Its action is not under Cabinet control, and the party affiliations of a majority of its members may be quite different from the affiliations of a majority of the House of Commons. Indeed, the intention of the fathers of the Canadian federation was to create a legislative body which would not be merely a replica of the lower house. The Senate, it was hoped, would protect provincial interests, would act as a revising body on measures passed by the Commons, and would give special representation to property and to the more conservative influences in the nation.

CONSTITUTIONAL PROVISIONS

Since the Senate was formed to embody the federal idea of a union of provinces, its membership was apportioned so as to recognize the interests of the provinces as separate units in the Dominion. This was not carried to the same lengths as in the United States (where each state has an equal number of senators), but the smaller provinces were nevertheless given proportionally greater representation than in the Commons. In 1948 representation in the Senate was based on four major divisions of the Dominion, each being assigned 24 members: Ontario; Quebec; the three Maritime Provinces (Nova Scotia, 10; New Brunswick, 10; Prince Edward Island, 4); and the four western provinces (6 each). The entry of Newfoundland in 1949 upset this balance. The new province was given 6 senators, and the four Maritime Provinces have now 30 seats. The total membership is therefore 102. A special provision (as amended) in the British North America Act, however, allows this maximum number to be increased under certain conditions to 106 or 110 (one or two extra members from each of the four divisions), the purpose of this flexibility being to give an opportunity to break a possible deadlock if a serious disagreement should arise between the Senate and the House of Commons.

Senators are appointed by the Governor-General-in-Council, and they hold office for life. They must reside in the province they represent, and if they happen to come from Quebec they must each represent a particular senatorial district in that province. A senator may belong to either sex; he must be at least thirty years old and a British subject; he must own real property within his province to a net value of $4,000, and be worth at least $4,000 over and above all debts and liabilities. A senator vacates his seat by losing his residence or property qualifications, by failing to attend the Senate for two consecutive sessions, by being convicted of any infamous crime, and on several other grounds. He is paid a salary of $6,000 a year.

PERSONNEL

Appointments to the Senate are, of course, really determined by the Prime Minister, and party service has in practice been the indispensable and in some instances the only qualification for a seat. The relative insignificance of the Senate as a legislative body gives it little appeal, however, for an active and ambitious man, so that the appointments are most attractive to those whose political life is almost over and who are looking for a sinecure for their declining years. Two recent examples will illustrate the point. In 1945 thirty-three, or over one-third of the members of the Senate, had been over 60 at the time of their appointment. On December 1, 1948, two new appointments were announced: one of these was 70 years of age, the other 74.

The Senate receives its share, and perhaps more than its share, of talent, for many of its members have had distinguished careers. In 1945, for example, the Senate contained twelve ex-Cabinet Ministers and ten ex-Ministers from provincial Cabinets. While able members of this type would normally be a credit to any legislative body, they are not likely to add lustre to the Senate; for during their genuinely useful period they are not in the upper house, but are busily acquiring credits which will later bring them a secure retirement at a substantial salary.

It is obvious that the advanced age of a large number of the senators is not occasioned by the fact of late appointment alone; the life tenure would in itself tend to produce a personnel well over the age of active service. A normal age for retirement in many businesses or professions is 65; yet in 1945, no less than 54 out of 95 senators, or 57 per cent, had reached this age of superannuation. On two occasions, indeed, Canada has had the questionable distinction of possessing a senator who had exceeded the mature age of 100 years.

The effect of this age factor on senatorial energy and initiative is well-nigh inescapable, and it applies both to the talented members and to those of lesser gifts. Senators remain in office regardless of their quality, their zeal, or the contribution they are able or willing to make to the business in hand. Here are no stirrings of ambition; no careers to be made; no governments to be overthrown; no honours to be sought; no driving spur to public service. "I have today signed my warrant of political death", wrote Sir George

Foster on his appointment to the Senate. "How colourless the Senate—the entering gate to coming extinction."

The fact that Canadian Cabinets have tended to stay in office for lengthy periods has had an important effect on the political complexion of the Senate, for the chamber has on several occasions come too much under the influence of one party. Thus in January, 1949, in a Senate of 96, there were 65 Liberal and 16 Opposition members; the 15 vacancies, when filled, would give a Liberal membership of 80. This Liberal preponderance would be certain to continue to increase until at least the next general election. Senators by the very conditions of their appointment are not likely to be impartial, and this partiality is made more pronounced by one party greatly outnumbering all others in the chamber. Minority parties, it may be added, have no chance of securing representation in the upper house. Despite the fact that since 1921 Alberta has consistently elected all its provincial governments and the great majority of its members in the House of Commons from minority parties, the Alberta senators during this entire period have been either Liberals or Conservatives.

POWERS AND FUNCTIONS

The chief function of the Senate is legislation, that is, the consideration and passage of bills which it either originates or receives from the House of Commons. The legislative procedure which is followed is broadly that used in the lower house (which is discussed in a later chapter), although the Senate lays more stress on its committee work and less on formal debate. One part of its activity is devoted to private bills. Most of this work takes place in committee, and is cheerfully relinquished by the Commons, for which these matters have little interest. The Senate also discusses resolutions on various questions which seem to be of general concern, but the educational value of such debates on public opinion is slight because the public itself rarely displays any interest in the Senate proceedings. Special committees of the Senate conduct investigations on specific topics or proposed legislation, on which occasions they gather evidence, interrogate witnesses, and submit reports of their findings. Some of these proceedings, while not directly legislative, are nevertheless highly desirable, for they prepare the way for future legislative action.

The Senate has always occupied a decidedly inferior position in relation to the House of Commons, and its comparative ineffectiveness has been accentuated by the tendency of the Cabinet to treat the Senate as of little consequence. The provision in the British North America Act (Section 53) whereby all bills for raising or spending money must originate in the Commons gave the real power to the elected representative body, and assurance has been made doubly sure by the custom that the Cabinet is always responsible to the Commons and never to the Senate.

The Senate was nevertheless able to maintain a limited prestige during the first forty or fifty years of its existence. One vital contributing factor was the practice of choosing two or more Ministers from its ranks, with the result that the Senate was able to keep in close touch with the Cabinet. Sir Robert Borden, however, began the new era of having in the Senate no Ministers who were heads of departments, and this has become since 1921 an accepted custom of the constitution. Inevitably very few Government measures are now introduced in the Senate, and the most valuable points of contact with the Cabinet have been removed. For while the Leader of the Government in the Senate may serve as the mouthpiece of the Cabinet, he is quite incapable of providing the necessary information on all the many subjects on which the Senate desires enlightenment. In 1948 an attempt was made to overcome this difficulty in some measure by allowing a Cabinet Minister (with a seat in the Commons) to appear and speak in the Senate, though not, of course, to vote;

but this procedure was used only once and is not likely to commend itself to a busy and overworked Cabinet.

The Senate has frequently opposed the House of Commons on legislation. While it has been much more disposed to *reject* bills from the lower house when under the control of a party which was not in a majority in the House, its tendency to *amend* bills has not been noticeably affected by party influences. Despite its independent position, it has not been indifferent to the popular will, and it has even gone so far as to acquiesce in the passage of a bill of which it disapproved simply because public opinion on the measure had been decisively expressed at a general election. Lacking clear evidence of the state of public opinion, however, the Senate has felt justified in using its own judgment and has amended and rejected bills freely.

The question whether the Senate has the constitutional power to amend a money bill has long been a matter of dispute between the two houses. The House of Commons, relying on the British parallel of the House of Lords, has always insisted that the Senate possessed no such power. The Senate, on the other hand, has never accepted this in theory, and in practice has repeatedly made its point, even amending bills which have dealt exclusively with matters of finance. In these cases the House has often accepted the amendments, but has added the quite futile proviso that they were not to be considered as constituting a precedent.

In summary, it may be said that the Senate, although severely handicapped, has been able to do some genuinely useful work. It revises and checks legislation sent up from the Commons; it conducts occasional investigations of undoubted merit; it takes by far the greater part of the load of private bill legislation from the overworked Commons. It has, however, not been a conspicuous success in guarding the rights of provincial or other minorities, although this was one of the chief reasons for its creation. Its attitude on social legislation has often been criticized as reactionary, but the evidence on this point is conflicting. The Senate, in short, has its merits, although they fall far short of justifying its continuance in its present form.

REFORM

The reform or abolition of the Senate has for many years provided the material for lively debate. A party which has few or no members in the Senate will always ardently demand a change; but no sooner does it gain power and acquire the major influence in the chamber than it discovers unsuspected virtues in the much abused body. A Government finds Senate appointments most useful as rewards for duty faithfully performed, as influences to produce immediate activity in the hope of recognition in the future, as inducements to persuade members of the Commons to resign and vacate a seat for new or defeated Cabinet Ministers, as aids for keeping restless provinces or provincial governments in line, and as a convenient scrap-heap on which to cast Ministers who have outlived their usefulness or who have become for one reason or another trying colleagues to retain in the Cabinet. Most of the smaller provinces, too, feel that their lot is a little more bearable with a few extra advocates in the Senate, even though these advocates may say little and may exercise a negligible influence on government policy.

The most important impediment to reform, perhaps, is the number and diversity of the plans which have been submitted as possible cures. No solution has been able to gain more than a few scattered supporters and even these have rarely shown any burning conviction. The Senate will in all likelihood continue to exist as at present constituted for many years to come, not from any high esteem in which it is held, but largely because of its undoubted convenience to the dominant political party and the general indifference of the Canadian people.

CHAPTER NINE

The House of Commons: Representation and Personnel

THE House of Commons is the body which above all others represents the people of Canada. It therefore speaks, as no other part of the government can pretend to speak, for the people. It is through the House of Commons that the will of the democracy finds expression and is made effective, and it is for this reason that the House is not only the primary legislative authority but also the body to which the Cabinet must constantly turn for approval.

FUNCTIONS OF THE HOUSE

The outstanding characteristic of the House is therefore its representative character. It is expected to reflect with approximate accuracy the ideas and wishes of the different races, classes, religions, and other groups into which the country is divided, and yet at the same time recognize the overriding interest of the nation as a whole. The composition of the House and the manner of its election forces it to keep in constant touch with the people it represents. Moreover, the fact that it is not a body of brilliant experts, but a fair sampling of the best of an average run, enables its members to speak for the electorate with genuine authority and understanding. The Cabinet thus finds the House an invaluable means of retaining contact with fluctuations in public opinion, for the members of the House can never allow themselves to drift very far away from the ultimate source of all political power.

The House of Commons, while performing its very important function of reflecting public opinion, must also in considerable measure lead and educate it, and the two processes of leading and following are always operative. The public must of necessity be ill-informed on many matters; and as the House dare not advance too far beyond what the people want, it finds itself frequently considering, debating, and investigating many matters, not with the purpose of arriving at an immediate decision, but rather of gradually preparing the minds of the people for policies which will come up for possible adoption in the future. Thus a proposal to reform the civil service, or to adopt a new system of voting, or to regulate election expenditures may be debated for several sessions and perhaps investigated by committees of the House before it is finally passed and takes its place in the statute book.

While the House must make many decisions, it is not primarily an initiating body: its function is essentially one of review, approval, and criticism. The Cabinet initiates, the House (and, to a much less degree, the Senate) takes the proposals and subjects them to a thorough examination before giving its assent. A casual observer, influenced by the very rare occasions on which the House forces amendments on the Cabinet, might suppose that this power of criticism is rarely effective; but such a conclusion would be superficial. The supporters of the Government acquiesce in its proposals because they have already exerted their influence within the party caucus, and their best endeavours are therefore devoted to expediting the passage of these proposals through the Commons. The Opposition's attacks on Government measures may seem to be futile, but the results of its efforts are not necessarily visible in the House. Some of these efforts will not, indeed, bear fruit until the next election. However, many of the possible objections of the Opposition were considered by the Government when drafting its bills, and these bills have in all probability already been toned down in anticipation of the criticisms which the Cabinet expected to be raised in the legislature. For it can be assumed that no Government willingly gives to the Opposition any ammunition which can be effectively used to its detriment either in Parliament or in the country.

The House of Commons also supervises much of the work of the Cabinet; and day after day the Opposition members ask questions, plan attacks, voice grievances, demand explanations, and generally subject the administration to disparaging scrutiny. The nation depends on the House to ensure an honest and efficient administration, and the chamber responds by keeping the Cabinet under fire at all times. As a last resort, the House can declare its lack of confidence in the Cabinet, and thus force a resignation or dissolution. Once again, however, the efficacy of the method must not be judged by what is directly accomplished; it depends rather on the Cabinet's knowledge that the supervisory duties of the House will be vigorously performed and that the surest defence is to give little cause for effective attack.

Finally, the Commons singles out ability and supplies a most valuable preparation for future Cabinet members. The great majority of the Ministers come from the House and serve their apprenticeship there; and the capacity of the potential Minister is in large measure judged by his performance as a private member. There is general agreement that no other kind of preliminary preparation is as effective as years spent in the House of Commons. New Cabinet members, while in a sense untrained, nevertheless come to their task with a valuable background of experience which serves as a very satisfactory substitute.

The formal decisions made by the House of Commons are of four kinds: (1) statutes or acts of Parliament; (2) the imposition of taxes and the authorization of expenditures, which are really only a special kind of statute; (3) resolutions, such as those requesting the British Parliament to amend the British North America Act, or those calling upon the Governor-in-Council to remove a judge; (4) formal declarations of state policy, which are not self-operating, but which the executive will certainly carry into effect, such as those dealing with treaties or the declaration of war.

REPRESENTATION

Representation in the House of Commons is based on population and is apportioned by provinces. An adjustment is made every ten years after the census has been taken. For almost eighty years the scheme of apportionment hinged on Quebec, which was given a fixed number of 65 members, while those from other provinces varied proportionately as their populations changed in relation to that of Quebec. One provision in the British North America Act, however, was found to work unfairly, and in 1946 a new system was introduced by an amendment to the Act whereby the total number of seats is fixed and representation of all provinces, subject to one exceptional provision (see (3) below), varies with population.

The results of the new system are as follows (the method of arriving at the results has been omitted):

1. The total number of members in the House is fixed at 262.

2. One member is given to the Yukon and Mackenzie Territories combined.

3. Four members are given to Prince Edward Island under a special amendment to the British North America Act in 1915, whereby no province shall have fewer members in the Commons than in the Senate.

4. The balance of members is distributed among the remaining provinces according to population, the larger remainders (which are left after the quota[1] is divided into a

[1] A brief, but incomplete, statement of method is necessary. The quota is obtained by dividing the population of all the provinces to be represented by the total seats available to those provinces. The result thus represents the ideal or normal number of people entitled to a representative—at present, 45,578. The quota is then divided into the population of each province to determine its representation.

The House of Commons: Representation

province's population) being used to fill in any vacancies. This yields the following results:

REDISTRIBUTION UNDER 1946 AMENDMENT (1941 CENSUS)

Province	Members under quota	Remainder after dividing by quota	Extra members through remainder	Total
P.E.I.	2	(2 more added under para. (3) above)		4
N.S.	12	31,026	1	13
N.B.	10	1,621	0	10
Que.	73	4,688	0	73
Ont.	83	4,681	0	83
Man.	16	496	0	16
Sask.	19	30,010	1	20
Alta.	17	21,343	0	17
B.C.	17	43,035	1	18
Yukon and Mackenzie	0	(1 given under para. (2) above)		1
Total	249	3	3	255
Newfoundland (1949 Amendment admitting Newfoundland)				7
			Total	262

FRANCHISE AND ELECTIONS

All but four of the members of the House of Commons are elected from constituencies which return only one member. Two constituencies (Halifax, and Queens, P.E.I.) each elect two members. The candidate who receives the highest number of votes is declared elected; and it is therefore possible that if more than two candidates are running in single-member districts, a member may be elected on a minority of votes. Thus in the general election of 1945, 965 candidates contested 245 seats, and 59 per cent of those who were successful had the support of only a minority of those voting.

The Canadian Parliament decides who shall **vot**e at Dominion elections. Generally speaking, any man or woman may vote if he or she is 21 years of age, a British subject, and complies with certain residential requirements. Certain persons, however, may be disqualified for special reasons, such as, the presiding officer in each constituency (except for a casting vote in event of a tie); all judges appointed by the Dominion; lunatics; prison inmates; those found guilty of corrupt or illegal practices at an election, and others.

A candidate will almost invariably secure a nomination by a political party,[1] so as to receive its support at the election. Certain legal steps are, however, also necessary to ensure that his name is placed on the ballot. He must be nominated by ten qualified voters who must comply with certain simple formalities and deposit $200. The deposit will be returned if the candidate is elected or receives at least one-half the number of votes cast for the successful candidate. If only one candidate is formally nominated, he is declared elected by acclamation.

The ballot contains no party identification whatever, but only the names of the candidates, their addresses, and occupations. Voting is secret; and no voter may cast any more than one vote.

If the results of an election are challenged on account of bribery or other cause, the dispute is taken to the courts, where two supreme court judges decide the case. It may then be appealed to the Supreme Court of Canada.

If a vacancy occurs between general elections because of death, resignation, or other cause, a special contest or by-election is held to choose a new member. These by-elections are frequently very important. Not only may the result alter the party balance in the House, but the election gives to both the Government and Opposition an opportunity to test their strength at the polls. A series of by-elections thus becomes a fairly reliable indication of the results which might ensue if a general election were to take place. Time and again Government policies have been substantially modified because of the significant trends in public opinion which a number of by-elections have revealed.

[1]See p. 127.

QUALIFICATIONS

The qualifications of a member of the House of Commons are simple: he (or she) must be a British subject and 21 years of age. He is, however, disqualified if he is a senator, a member of a provincial legislature, a government contractor, the holder of a salaried government position (other than that of a Minister) and for several other reasons. A member is not legally required to live in his constituency, although there is a tendency for most members to do so.

TERM AND SALARY

There is no definite term for a member of the House, except that it cannot exceed five years. Inasmuch as Parliament can be dissolved and a new election held at any time, the term may be anything from a month or two up to the maximum. The usual life of a Parliament, however, is about four years. No Cabinet is anxious to bring about an election before it is necessary; though on the other hand, no Cabinet wishes to have the date of the election fixed by the calendar, for there is a decided advantage to be gained if the Government is able to select what it considers to be an appropriate time and suitable issues for the contest. While this variable factor adds an undesirable element of uncertainty to elections, it has the great merit of frequently obtaining an immediate electoral verdict on urgent public questions.

A member of the House is paid $4,000 a session with an additional $2,000 a year which is exempt from income tax. Cabinet Ministers and the Leader of the Opposition receive $18,000 a year; the Prime Minister, $23,000.

PARLIAMENTARY PRIVILEGE

Members of both Canadian houses enjoy special "privileges" which are copied from those of the British Parliament.

Some of these are derived from usage, but the great majority rest on statutes which have transplanted the privileges of the British Parliament to the Canadian Senate and House of Commons. The British North America Act (as amended in 1875) gives the Canadian Parliament the power to acquire by statute all the privileges which are enjoyed by the British Parliament at the time such statute is enacted.

Individual members, for example, have complete freedom of speech in their capacity as members and they cannot be prosecuted in any court for anything which they have said in the House or in its committees. A member cannot be assaulted or intimidated in the House or in going to or from the House; nor can he be arrested for certain minor offences while Parliament is in session or for some time before and after the parliamentary session.

The House also enjoys collective privileges as a legislative body. It has the power to preserve order and discipline in all its proceedings, and also to punish anyone outside the House who is guilty of making scandalous or libellous statements concerning its proceedings or its members. It may also refuse to seat a person who has been duly elected as a member, and it has power to expel any member of the House.

While some of these privileges may seem excessively generous, the main purpose is clear and free from any serious objection. It is highly desirable, for example, that the member should be given every inducement to express himself freely and not be subjected in the performance of his duty to any kind of intimidation from any source. It is also imperative that the House should be able to conduct its business in a seemly and orderly fashion. While it is true that certain of these privileges may sometimes be misused, the risk of an occasional misuse is far preferable to the dangers which would be likely to occur if these exceptional powers and safeguards were removed.

CHAPTER TEN

The House of Commons: Legislation

THE House of Commons meets in a rectangular chamber with the Speaker seated on a dais at one of the narrow ends. The members of the Government party occupy the long side of the chamber at the right of the Speaker; while the Opposition parties face them on the other long side. The Prime Minister sits in the front row of the Government desks about one-third of the way down the chamber from the Speaker, and is flanked by his Cabinet Ministers. The Leader of the Opposition, supported by his chief assistants, is directly opposite; and the other Opposition parties form their own little groups about their leaders. The Clerk of the House and the Clerk-Assistant sit at the table of the House in front of the Speaker. The mace, the symbol of the Speaker's authority, rests on top of the table when the Speaker is in the chair. The official reporters are midway between the Speaker and the entrance or "bar" of the House, guarded by the Sergeant-at-Arms. Galleries occupy all four sides of the chamber.

The Speaker is elected for each Parliament, that is, at the first meeting of the House after a general election. He is a member of the House and is always chosen from the ranks of the majority party. French-speaking and English-speaking Speakers alternate, although occasionally a Speaker may be re-elected by the next Parliament. The Deputy Speaker, who presides over the House in Committee, must possess a "full and practical knowledge" of the language which is not that of the Speaker, a provision which ensures a French- and English-speaking alternation in this office also. The duties of the Speaker are to preside over the meetings of the House, to interpret and apply the rules, to maintain discipline and decorum, to defend the rights and privileges of the House and its members, and to represent the House on all formal occasions.

RULES OF THE HOUSE

An earlier chapter has shown that the Cabinet exercises very great authority in legislation, and some indication was given of the way in which the party majority and discipline make such authority effective. But both the Cabinet and the private members are subject to the rules of the House in the attainment of their ends, and little mention has yet been made of the way in which the House conducts its formal business. The rules are quite impartial and are designed to protect the rights of all members, irrespective of party. Although the Government's majority is bound to give it a definite advantage, the Opposition parties still have ample opportunity under the rules to present their views and criticisms at more than reasonable length. It is, however, not without significance that the most frequent openings for attacking the Government do not occur on Opposition bills or resolutions but rather at the time when the Government is endeavouring to pass its measures through the House.

The rules of the House set aside certain days of the week for the special use of the Government and of private members respectively, and a glance at this distribution of time gives the impression that the private members have been treated very generously. But this nominal distribution alters greatly as the session advances. After a number of weeks the House (on the motion of a Cabinet Minister) invariably decides to give Government business precedence on certain of the periods allotted to private members, and these encroachments eventually become so extensive that almost all the time set aside for the use of private members disappears. The Opposition members make a formal protest, but they nevertheless accept the restriction with a good grace, for they recognize that only by giving priority to Government business can the House hope to deal with the Government's programme within the time available in an ordinary session. The inevitable result is that private member bills and resolutions rarely progress very far in the House. They do not fail because of an adverse vote, but because the debate is rarely finished within the time allotted for discussion, and there is therefore no opportunity for a vote to be taken. Many private member bills and resolutions, indeed, never come up for discussion at all, for they are crowded off the agenda by other business.

The rules which cover the debates also tend in actual operation to favour the Government, for they restrict prolonged discussion and thereby turn the edge of the Opposition's most useful weapon. Thus the rule which limits most speeches to forty minutes' duration does not help the Opposition, for they have plenty of time to waste, but it proves almost indispensable to the Government which must place a large number of legislative measures on the statute book in the space of a few months. Another threat to unrestricted speech is the closure, a device to terminate debate and force a speedy vote. The Cabinet uses this club sparingly, for it is always afraid of being accused of suppressing discussion. Yet the knowledge that the closure is available and may be invoked at any time is not without effect on a talkative Opposition.

It must not be supposed that the members of the Government and Opposition parties conduct the business of Parliament in an atmosphere of hate and distrust. Debates are rarely bitter, and the parties consult and co-operate amicably with one another in making many informal arrangements for the greater convenience of all. Each party has its own "whips" or members who are in charge of inter-party negotiations and understandings, such as the "pairing" of members,[1] the selection of members for committees, and the provision of speakers for debates. A spirit of compromise and fairness usually prevails; and the parliamentary struggle is regarded in large measure as a game among contestants who derive a common advantage from seeing that the general amenities are preserved.

THE PASSAGE OF BILLS

A public bill in order to become an act or statute must go through three readings in the House and three in the Senate before it receives the assent of the Governor-General. If the bill originates in the Senate, the order of the passage through the two houses is reversed. If a bill is amended by either house, the bill, as amended, must be accepted by the other before going to the Governor-General. If agreement is not reached, the bill is, of course, lost.

The legislative process involves, however, many more steps than the seven basic ones named above. The following account, while far from complete, will indicate in somewhat greater detail the passage of a public bill through the House of Commons.

The *first reading* of a public bill[2] is a formality, and is in effect little more than information given to the House that the bill is on its way. No debate or amendment is permitted.

The *second reading* is the most important stage in a bill's passage, and debate here may be full and prolonged. It is confined to the discussion of the general principles of the bill; for the question which the House is to decide at this time is whether there is a need for a bill at all and whether the broad purposes of this particular measure are sound.

If the House approves of the bill in principle and gives it a second reading, the next step is to consider its details in

---

[1] A member who wishes to absent himself from Parliament for a few days is "paired" with a member of another party, and during that stated period neither will vote in a party division.

[2] Bills which involve the expenditure of money or the imposition of a tax must pass a *resolution stage* before coming up for the first reading.

committee. The House now wishes to find out whether the particular provisions proposed will best achieve the ends which have already been accepted as desirable. To obtain an answer to this question, the bill may pursue several alternative courses.

1. It may go to the *Committee of the Whole House.* This is simply the entire House sitting as a large committee. The membership is unchanged; but the chamber uses different and more informal rules of procedure. The Chairman of Committees, and not the Speaker, presides; the mace is removed from the top of the table and placed out of sight; members may speak any number of times on a measure; speeches are likely to be short and to the point; and members customarily address questions and answers directly to one another rather than through the chairman. At this stage any discussion of the principles of the bill is out of order, and the Committee takes it up literally clause by clause, and accepts, rejects, or amends them one by one.

2. It may go to a *Select Committee* which is specially appointed by the House for the purpose of investigating the subject with which the bill deals and obtaining further information before a decision is taken.

3. It may go to one of a number of *Standing Committees* of the House. These are committees set up each session on certain broad topics, Agriculture and Colonization, Industrial Relations, Banking and Commerce, etc. The House follows no consistent practice in its use of these Standing Committees: some of them may not meet during the entire session; others may be kept fairly busy. Representation (and this is true of Select Committees as well) is allotted to the different parties in proportion to the number of their members in the House, so that the Government is in a majority on all committees. The bill will naturally be sent to the Standing Committee on the general field within which the measure lies.

Even if the bill follows route (2) or (3), it will still come back and travel over (1) to receive consideration by the

Committee of the Whole. From here it is reported to the House itself, which may accept or reject any amendments which have been made in Committee. If there are no amendments from the Committee of the Whole, this *report stage* is omitted.

Finally, the bill will come up for its *third reading*, which is usually not a very formidable hurdle to surmount. Amendments may be offered, but the debate is almost invariably short. If it passes this reading, it is sent on to the Senate, where procedure is much the same as in the Commons.

FINANCE

A very large part of the attention of the House is concentrated on financial legislation—bills to authorize the spending of money or, as they are called, "supply"; and bills to authorize the raising of money by taxes of all kinds, or "ways and means".

Months before the supply bill appears in Parliament each government department is busily engaged in preparing its estimated expenditures for the coming year. These are carefully scrutinized (and probably cut down) by the deputy minister and the Minister, then reviewed by the staff of the Treasury Board, then pruned by the Treasury Board itself,[1] and finally approved by the Cabinet. The Minister of Finance transmits all these "estimates" (those of each department being separately grouped) to the House, and they go at once to the *Committee of Supply*. This is simply the Committee of the Whole House functioning in a special capacity for the consideration of the estimates.

The House in Committee of Supply considers the estimates, department by department, and broken down into compara-

---

[1] The Treasury Board is a statutory committee of the Privy Council composed of the Minister of Finance, as chairman, and five other Ministers, with the Deputy Minister of Finance as secretary. It exercises very extensive authority in all financial matters. Its small size, the ability and prominence of its members, and the fact that the Minister of Finance (who has the responsibility for raising all revenues) is the chairman, make the Board unusually effective in keeping down expenditures.

tively small items, over a period of several months. These items are printed side by side with the corresponding appropriations for the current year which were voted in the previous session of Parliament, in order that the members of the House may be able to compare the two and discuss the proposals more intelligently. Whenever an opportunity appears in the time allotted to the Government, it is used to bring forward and push through a batch of estimates. A Minister moves that the House go into Committee of Supply; and he then calls up, explains, and defends the estimates for his department. It will be recalled that no private member can move to have any of these estimates increased; but anyone may move to have them decreased or struck out.

After each of the departmental resolutions or "votes" for spending money have been separately approved in Committee, the Minister of Finance introduces in the House an omnibus Supply bill which includes them all. This bill is then passed through the usual stages in the House and emerges eventually as the Appropriation Act.

The other side of the financial picture is revenue. This centres about the budget, which is brought down by the Minister of Finance well along in the session. In his budget speech the Minister endeavours to weigh the probable revenue from existing taxes and other sources of income against the known and estimated expenditure; and he presents proposals to bring the two in balance. If a surplus is indicated, substantial reductions in taxes may be made; if a deficit, then this must be met by tax adjustments, tax increases, new taxes, or capital borrowings. The budget speech is made on a motion that the House go into *Committee of Ways and Means*. This is a third manifestation of the Committee of the Whole House and the one which is concerned with raising money. When the House goes into Committee, it proceeds to consider the resolutions which contain the proposals made by the Minister of Finance. They are eventually passed, are embodied in one or more bills (a tariff bill, a bill to amend the Income Tax Act, etc.) and then go through the usual stages necessary for public bill legislation.

A major responsibility of the Cabinet is the authorizing, auditing, and checking of all public accounts. These are under the special direction of the Treasury Board, and are entrusted for the most part to the Comptroller of the Treasury, who maintains a network of accounting branches throughout all departments. A further check is supplied by the Auditor-General, who is an official of Parliament—not of the Cabinet—and who reports annually to Parliament on any irregularity, exceptional procedure, or other matter concerning the public finances which he considers worthy of its attention. Parliament may then in the light of this report take whatever action it deems advisable.

CHAPTER ELEVEN

The House of Commons and the Cabinet

THE foregoing account has indicated the marked ascendancy of the Cabinet over the House of Commons. The Cabinet (through the Governor-General) summons, prorogues, and dissolves the House; it exercises a tremendous influence over all legislation and virtually complete power over financial legislation; it controls the time, regulates the business, and apportions the energies of the House for almost every hour of the parliamentary session. The House of Commons would thus seem to have degenerated into little more than a ratifying body for Cabinet proposals, a representative chamber which the Cabinet uses as a convenient screen to hide its exercise of supreme political authority. The Cabinet has apparently ceased to be responsible to the Commons; the Commons has to all intents and purposes become responsible to the Cabinet.

While this is an over-simplification and an exaggeration of the actual condition, it contains a substantial amount of truth. The executive, of course, must always be the initiator and the chief agent of government, although it should admittedly function under the searching regard of an alert and critical House. But the House itself needs leadership, for if left alone it will fritter its time away in futile and pointless discussion. Its attention and efforts must be guided and constantly brought back to the major issues. Much wrangling and repetition and pointless discussion are unavoidable and cannot and should not be suppressed, but these must be kept within bounds and never allowed to become the chief end of Parliament. The role of the Cabinet is thus a double one. It is responsible for the production of proposals to deal with the current problems of government, and it is also responsible for giving guidance to the Commons, which looks to it for legislative as well as executive leadership.

This situation need not lead nor has it in fact led to the abdication of the House of Commons; for the House may still wield a substantial influence over the Cabinet. The extent of that influence is admittedly difficult to gauge, but no Cabinet Minister could be found who would question its potency or deny that it had a very real effect on Government policies and the conduct of parliamentary business. The House controls the Cabinet—rarely by defeating it, often by criticizing it, still more often by the Cabinet's discounting the criticism before subjecting itself and its acts to the House, and always by the latent capacity of the chamber to revolt against its leaders. Evidence of this is unmistakable in the activities of the House under different conditions. A House with a weak Opposition is almost certain to prove lethargic, careless, and discursive, for the Government is secure and its assailants ineffective. A House which contains a powerful and aggressive Opposition, ably led, feels the quickening and wholesome effect of that infusion throughout all its proceedings.

OPPORTUNITIES FOR CRITICISM

What means are available to the private members, and particularly to those in the Opposition, to develop their criticisms and to place their views before the House and the nation? To a marked degree the Opposition will make its own openings for the expression of its opinions. These will occur chiefly at the different stages in the legislative process, for many of these stages form admirable points from which skilful and effective attacks can be conducted. The rules of the House, however, present many other opportunities which are designed and preserved for the especial purpose of allowing the members of the House to gain information, to prod the Ministers into activity, and to present arguments for and against the Government's policies. Six of these major opportunities are briefly described below.

1. At the opening of each session the Governor-General reads the Speech from the Throne, a concise statement (passed by the Cabinet) setting forth the chief measures which the Government proposes to bring before Parliament during the ensuing months. An address is moved in the House by two Government supporters in reply to the Speech from the Throne, and every member may participate in the debate which follows. There is virtually no limit to the subject-matter, and this debate therefore furnishes an exceptionally wide opening for discursive discussion on all topics.

2. An opportunity is given at the beginning of most sittings of the House for the members to address questions to the Minister concerning virtually anything which comes under the control of the Dominion government. The question must be simple and direct, and neither it nor the answer is debatable. The ability to question the Government in this way is an invaluable privilege, for it enables the Opposition to keep in close touch with the administration and to draw out many hidden matters into the light of day. A number of safeguards have been raised against abuse of this interrogation; but, generally speaking, the Minister is not allowed to withhold any information which is requested unless he can plead that to give it would be contrary to the public interest. Plans for measures of national defence, for example, frequently fall in this category.

3. The rules provide that an urgent matter can be brought before the House for immediate discussion (subject to certain conditions) on a motion to adjourn to discuss "a definite matter of urgent public importance". The debate which follows will not only draw attention to the event or complaint

in question, but almost certainly will necessitate a reply by a Minister and perhaps a statement of Government policy as well.

4. The custom grew up in England hundreds of years ago that when the King asked Parliament for money, Parliament would use the occasion to demand a redress of its grievances against the Crown. A similar opportunity occurs today in the Canadian House of Commons when a Minister moves that the House go into Committee of Supply or Committee of Ways and Means; at such a time any member of the House may bring up virtually any subject and have it debated forthwith.

5. The budget furnishes yet another wide opportunity for members to talk about anything that lies nearest their hearts. The budget speech of the Minister of Finance covers a wide variety of subjects, including both national and international affairs, and the debate which follows will therefore allow all members to discuss anything which falls within these extensive fields or, indeed, anything which might conceivably be considered to be remotely connected with them.

6. A defeat of a Government measure indicates that the Government does not possess the confidence of the House; but it is always possible to move an explicit motion of want of confidence. This would seem to be the most obvious method of attacking the Cabinet, but the other opportunities are usually more convenient and are also so numerous that there is rarely any need for the direct vote. A formal challenge by the Leader of the Opposition, however, will always be accepted quickly by the Cabinet, a debate will be arranged, and in due course the motion of lack of confidence will be defeated or passed.

It is therefore evident that while the Cabinet will almost invariably have its measures accepted by Parliament, the private members (whether on the Government side or in the Opposition) need never complain that they have been denied

LEGISLATIVE BUILDINGS, EDMONTON

Alberta Government

ONTARIO PREMIER TAKING OATH OF OFFICE

Ontario Government

THE GRAND STAIRCASE, LEGISLATIVE BUILDINGS, WINNIPEG

Manitoba Government Travel and Publicity Bureau

a fair or lengthy hearing. While the rules of the House may be somewhat faulty in detail and beyond any doubt would be the better for partial revision, they nevertheless embody satisfactorily the two fundamental principles which are essential to democratic government. These are, first, that the Government should always be able to secure powers which are adequate to its task; second, that the minority, which is in opposition, should always be able to criticize fully and effectively any or all of the Government's policies.[1]

It has already been suggested that the basic condition under which the House operates is a genuine spirit of tolerance and fair play. The majority are usually unwilling, for example, to take undue advantage of the power which political fortune has temporarily placed in their hands. Indeed, time and again a party leader will be found to forego the momentary advantage and maintain a principle which strengthens the position of his adversary. A Cabinet Minister will frequently intervene on behalf of an opponent if he believes the ruling of the Speaker to be wrong or to have given insufficient weight to interparty arrangements which may have been agreed upon. The Leader of the Opposition will prove an even more zealous defender of the minority privileges, for his position—and interests—make him their especial guardian, and he will be as much concerned for the privileges of other minorities as for those of the party he leads.

Intervention on the part of a Cabinet Minister may not be, of course, all pure undiluted sportsmanship blended with a love of minority rights. No Government can be quite unmindful of the fact that in protecting the minority today, it is actually protecting itself tomorrow. This sober reflection is likely to introduce a kindly note into its relations with other parties. Moreover, no Government wishes to affront the basic political tolerance in the electorate, which would

[1] The balance of this chapter is taken with few changes from the author's *The Government of Canada* (University of Toronto Press, 1947).

resent, and in all likelihood actively resent, any flagrant interference with freedom of speech and criticism. Finally, the members of the minority always have their own defences, and a wise Cabinet will know that it can often persuade far more successfully than it can drive. "Is it the Government's fault," asked Mr. J. L. Ilsley, when Minister of Finance, "that so much discussion goes on, that it takes so many days to get through a particular item? I tried just before the Easter recess to crowd the House a little. I will not do it again. If the Government starts to crowd the House, the House crowds the Government. That always happens. The moment we indicate to the House that we want to get ahead, we simply precipitate speeches about the right of the House of Commons to discuss matters and to discuss them thoroughly."

THE STRUGGLE FOR POWER

But while the rules and customs of the House will protect the rights of the rival forces, they can win no engagements for them. All contestants must therefore be conditioned and disciplined and equipped for service. Here the parliamentary organization of the parties plays a very useful part. Some mention has already been made of the control which the Government is able to exercise over its members. It also has the tremendous advantage of having leaders who are in actual authority and not merely at the head of party councils. To a useful prestige they can add the very practical virtue of being in a position where they can dispense favours and consolidate power.

Ministerial leaders have also great ability at their disposal. They can draw freely on the talents of their civil servants, who will supply them with ideas, prepare and execute their programmes, and furnish the debating material necessary for their vindication. This assistance gives them a pronounced advantage as a fighting unit. For it is virtually impossible to draw any distinction between Ministers as Ministers and Ministers as party leaders, between the Government's proposals and the proposals of the majority party. It is therefore a wise party which allows a fairly free hand to its Ministers in office. The Ministers cannot help but be better informed than any party organization, although the latter may well play a useful part in furnishing the leaders with a special kind of information by keeping them in touch with public opinion.

An Opposition party is rarely so generously provided with leaders and never so well equipped with assistance as is the Government. This constitutes a serious handicap which affects not only the party in the narrow sense but also the efficacy of its legislative work, and from that, the work of Parliament as well. There is therefore very much to be said for the idea that each party should have a generous public grant (based on its membership in the Commons) for the sole purpose of financing research and allied services. A well-armed Opposition is no liability, but a national asset. If Canadian government accepts, as it does, the principle of paying the Leader of the Opposition a substantial salary to criticize the Government, it would seem only logical to give that Leader (and probably some other minority leaders as well) some assistance with which to render his criticism more effective.

It is sometimes asserted that the political struggle is carried to extremes, and that politics encourages a hyper-sensitivity to error, an exaggeration of issues, and a morbid suspicion of motives and purposes which often come close to absurdity. Yet these things are probably inescapable accompaniments of responsibility and good government. For the Cabinet remains efficient primarily because the searchlight of publicity never ceases to play upon it; and the Opposition directs the beams of the searchlight.

The final objective of the Opposition is a majority of seats in the House of Commons. This can rarely be obtained by the direct alienation of Government supporters in the House, but it can most certainly occur as the result of the next general election. At such a time the shifting of a small number of popular votes from one side to the other may bring about a change in Government, and the eyes of the Opposition are ever searching for material which will win over these detachable voters. The perpetual criticism, the amendments to motions, the divisions in the House, the tedious debates, the theatrical denunciations, the meticulous examination of the estimates, and scores of other manoeuvres have this as their ultimate goal; and no expedient or weapon is so insignificant that it can be neglected in the unceasing engagement for prestige, for reputation, and eventually for power.

The Government, for its part, must retain its existing majority and, whenever possible, extend it. While it has always the advantage of holding office and directing affairs, it also has the responsibility of exercising the initiative and of finding the remedies for the many ills that beset the country. The first essential is that it must get its measures and estimates through Parliament. Thus, while it must give the Opposition ample opportunity for criticism, it must also be continually pressing Parliament for action. "The Prime Minister is obliged," said Mr. Mackenzie King, "to keep constantly in mind two vital objectives: the one, to seek to provide opportunity for the fullest and frankest discussion of matters of public interest: the other, to see that sufficient time is provided for the full and proper discussion of the important business of government. It is a difficult and delicate task to hold the balance between the urgent demands of the Government upon the time of Parliament, and a proper regard for the privileges, so essential to the sound functioning of a free community, of the private members of Parliament." From this flows the paradox that a Government wants little verbal backing from its own supporters. What it needs most is "brute votes", and while some parliamentary defenders are necessary to uphold its course on the floors of the House, every speaker over that minimum simply impedes the passage of Government measures.

The Cabinet is compelled for its own sake to avoid even the appearance of defeat or of weakness. This is the chief reason behind its stiff and unyielding attitude to many excellent suggestions coming from the Opposition side. A few of these the Cabinet may be able to accept with dignity; but let this acquiescence become frequent, and the electorate will naturally conclude that the simpler solution would be to place in power the party which is so fertile in valuable ideas rather than acquire them in this circuitous fashion.

The need to preserve its strength also gives the clue to the indirect influence of criticism which has already been discussed. Criticism by the Opposition casts its shadow before: it invades the Cabinet meeting and the Government caucus; it is most influential before it is formally voiced. How will the Opposition attack this project? Will it be easier to defend next year than this? What will the farmers think of it? How will it affect the Government vote in Ontario? What will be the attitude of the leading Opposition newspapers? Objections will be anticipated as far as possible when the measure is being drafted, and the Cabinet will thereafter defend it ardently and refuse to accept any amendment of any consequence. If a serious flaw in the proposal is later discovered, the safest way of escape is to abandon it as unobtrusively as the circumstances (and the Opposition) will allow.

Parliament concentrates and dramatizes the struggle for political power by bringing the political parties into immediate and continual conflict. Arguments are marshalled on one side and on the other, criticism and counter-proposals are made in full publicity, and the reputation of one side mounts as that of another falls away. Elections do not catch the voter by surprise and quite unprepared for the ballot. The ground has been worked over beforehand, the prestige of the Government is frequently established or destroyed long before polling day, and even new issues find their place in an environment which is by no means unfamiliar. There is always an alternative Government, if one is needed, near at hand—one which will pick up the work of its predecessor, make a few alterations here, develop certain things there, adapt old institutions to new ideas, and gradually press on a bit further the tentative experiment in human relations which is the business of government.

CHAPTER TWELVE

The Judiciary

THE judiciary is primarily concerned with disputes which are brought to the courts for decision. The disputes may involve individuals or organizations or even one or more governments. A criminal action, for example, is brought against the offender by the Crown, which is simply the Government acting in the interests and on behalf of the public. In the course of giving its decisions the court ensures that the rule of law is maintained: that no one is punished except for a breach of the law; and that no government official exercises any power which the law does not authorize. The court protects the rights of citizens against one another and their rights against their government. If in the course of a dispute, one party should challenge the validity of a law or action passed or performed by a Dominion, provincial, or municipal authority, the court will inquire into the question of jurisdiction and declare the law or action within or beyond the powers of the authority concerned.

The courts in Canada will also give an opinion on stated questions which involve the interpretation of the British North America Act or the constitutionality of Dominion and provincial legislation, when they are required to do so by the Governor-General-in-Council or (in some provinces) by the Lieutenant-Governor-in-Council. These questions may be addressed to the Supreme Court of Canada (under a Dominion statute) or to a provincial Supreme Court (under a provincial statute). While no actual dispute has arisen, the Dominion and one or more provincial governments will usually be represented by counsel, and arguments will be presented on both sides. In this way a constitutional opinion is obtained from the courts without the delay which might be occasioned by awaiting the occurrence of a genuine dispute.

The federal Parliament has the power under the British North America Act to create a general court of appeal as well as "any additional courts for the better administration of the laws of Canada". The provincial legislatures have control over "the administration of justice in the province, including the constitution, maintenance, and organization of provincial courts, both of civil and criminal jurisdiction, and including procedure in civil matters in those courts". Procedure in criminal matters is under the Dominion, and it also appoints, pays, and, if necessary, removes (subject to minor exceptions) the judges of all Dominion and provincial courts.

THE SYSTEM OF COURTS

The system of courts in Canada is for the most part organized in pyramidal form, with a right of appeal (subject to numerous restrictions) running from the lower courts to those above. The courts are as follows:

1. *The Judicial Committee of the Privy Council.* This is primarily composed of British judges, although it also contains some judges from the Dominions. It was until very recently the highest court of appeal for Canadian cases. In 1933, however, appeals in all criminal cases were abolished by the Canadian Parliament, and all other appeals were stopped by another statute in 1949. The Supreme Court of Canada has thus become the court of final appeal.

2. *The Supreme Court of Canada.* This was established by Canadian statute in 1875. It is now composed of a Chief Justice and eight judges, appointed by the Governor-General-in-Council. They hold office during good behaviour, but must retire at seventy-five. They may be removed by the

THEIR MAJESTIES KING GEORGE VI AND QUEEN
ELIZABETH GIVE ROYAL ASSENT TO BILLS IN
SENATE CHAMBER, OTTAWA, 1939

PROCESSION FROM LEGISLATURE FOLLOWING
READING OF SPEECH FROM THRONE, HALIFAX

LEGISLATIVE BUILDING, REGINA

Saskatchewan Government

LEGISLATIVE COUNCIL, QUEBEC

Le Soleil

Governor-General-in-Council, following a joint address passed by both Houses of Parliament.

The court exercises general appellate jurisdiction; that is, it hears appeals from provincial courts and the Exchequer Court of Canada.

3. *Provincial Supreme Courts.* These vary greatly in size and organization with each province, the larger provinces clearly needing a more elaborate system. A province like Nova Scotia has one Supreme Court: the individual judges go on circuit, and they sit together as a court of appeal. In a large province like Ontario the Supreme Court consists of two divisions, a Court of Appeal and a High Court. The former is only concerned with appeals from the High Court or lower courts. The latter is primarily engaged in trying cases (both civil and criminal) when they first arise for settlement, although it may also hear a few appeals.

The judges of all provincial supreme courts are appointed by the Governor-General-in-Council and hold office during good behaviour. There is no compulsory retirement because of age.

4. *County Courts.* These exercise original jurisdiction in small disputes and have authority to try minor criminal offences. The judges are appointed by the Governor-General-in-Council during good behaviour, but must retire at the age of seventy-five.

5. *Minor provincial courts.* These are very numerous in the larger provinces. They include surrogate (or probate) courts, division courts, magistrates' courts, juvenile courts, courts of arbitration, etc. They are completely under provincial control both as to organization and maintenance, and as to appointment, remuneration, tenure, etc. For the most part these judicial officers hold office during good behaviour, and the provincial authority has the power of removal.

The Exchequer Court of Canada does not fit neatly into this hierarchy. It is a specialized Dominion court, created by federal statute, and consists at present of a President and four other judges. It hears cases involving the revenues of the Crown (notably taxation cases); cases concerning copyrights, patents, trade marks, etc.; admiralty cases; and others. Appeals normally lie to the Supreme Court of Canada. The judges are appointed by the Governor-in-Council, hold office during good behaviour (with compulsory retirement at seventy-five) and may be removed by the usual joint address procedure.

JUDICIAL SAFEGUARDS

It will be observed that the judges (with a very few exceptions at the magistrates' level) are given very special safeguards which are not usually accorded to other officials of the government.

1. They hold office during good behaviour, which means, in effect, for life or until they reach the age of retirement. "Good behaviour" is, moreover, interpreted generously, and only very scandalous conduct on the part of a Dominion or provincial supreme court judge would be accepted as a valid reason for putting him out of office. Misbehaviour as applied to a county court judge is a slightly more elastic term, and the protection given is not nearly so extreme.

2. A large number of the judges cannot be compelled to retire. The British North America Act gives to the judges of the supreme courts in the provinces a tenure during good behaviour, and Parliament has considered that compulsory retirement would violate this protection. Parliament has, however, provided for a stoppage of salary and a refusal of a pension if a judge of any Dominion or provincial court refuses to retire on pension when, after careful investigation, it is established that he is incapacitated by age or infirmity from carrying out his judicial duties. The tenure of judges of the Supreme and Exchequer Courts of Canada and the county courts is not covered by the British North America Act, and a Canadian statute compels these judges to retire at seventy-five.

3. The process of removal is elaborate and difficult to bring into action. All the Dominion and provincial supreme court judges are subject to removal by the Governor-General-in-Council after a joint address requesting such removal has been passed by the Senate and House of Commons. This has been made much more difficult to apply by the addition of a number of preliminary steps before the joint address, so that the effect of the entire procedure is to surround the position with almost insurmountable defences. County court judges are not as secure, for they may be removed, after investigation, by the Governor-General-in-Council.

POSITION OF THE JUDICIARY

There are, of course, very substantial reasons for the special treatment accorded the judiciary, and they are closely connected with the idea of division of powers as applied to this branch of government.[1] The functions of a judge are totally unlike those of most other government officials, and it is therefore considered highly undesirable to subject the judge to the same sanctions which are used against most of the other agents of government.

The essential prerequisite for the proper exercise of the judicial function is fairness and impartiality. These qualities assume a large degree of detachment from any influence which might disturb the delicate equipoise and scrupulous objectivity which the judge must try to preserve at all times. The judge must therefore be placed in a position of complete independence. He must be able to perform his duties conscientiously and without fear, and he must not be worried about the possible consequences of an unpopular or inconvenient decision. The opinions of the judge must be founded not on what people want, but rather on the law itself. The judge's decision emerges from the application of the legal principles to the facts.

[1] See p. 14.

The judge is thus not an agent of government who is trying to carry out a particular policy, and he is emphatically not subject to instruction by the people or their representatives in the rendering of his decisions. The ordinary relationships between the people and their representatives or between these representatives and their agents in the government simply do not exist here, and the enforcement of political responsibility (which is the secret of most legislative and executive efficiency) would, if applied to a judge, bring into play the very influences which must be rigorously excluded.

It is this need which furnishes the justification for a division of power which will isolate the courts and cut them off from political influences which might flow from the executive and legislative branches. If the judge is to be kept honest, conscientious, energetic, and fair-minded, other inducements than political responsibility must be used and other rewards and stimuli must be made available. The stronger the judge's position is made against interference and punishment, the greater is the need for stressing intangible and moral factors to preserve his integrity.

Unusual care, for example, should be taken at the time of his selection as a judge to ensure that he possesses both character and ability. Appointment by Governor-in-Council is not a perfect means to this end, but it has produced fairly satisfactory results. Even a sincere desire to make good appointments is not in itself enough; for their quality will depend on the degree to which the position can be made attractive to eminent members of the legal profession. Thus the salary paid the judge must be substantial,[1] without necessarily being extravagant. He must be so placed that bribery and similar influences will have little appeal, and he must be offered enough to induce him to leave a lucrative

---

[1] Salaries paid to Canadian judges vary with the court. Judges on the Supreme Court of Canada receive $16,000 ($20,000 for the Chief Justice); on the Supreme Court of Ontario, $12,000 ($13,333.33 for the Chief Justice); in the county courts $6,666.66 with additional remuneration for special judicial duties.

practice for the public service. The office, moreover, must be regarded as one of great honour and dignity; the social position must be assured; the rectitude, fairness, and character of the judge must invariably be assumed. No political or social device can possibly guarantee that a high degree of ability and integrity will always be obtained in any office, but such factors as those enumerated will make the securing of those qualities in a judge extremely probable. The fine record of the Canadian judiciary bears testimony to the accuracy of this belief.

CHAPTER THIRTEEN

Provincial Government

THE outstanding feature of governments of the Canadian provinces is the fact that they, no less than the federal government, have been largely modelled on English law and practice. Interesting evidence of this was recorded over a hundred years ago by Charles Dickens, who attended the opening of a session of the Nova Scotia legislature:

> It happened to be the opening of the Legislative Council and General Assembly, at which ceremonial the forms observed on the commencement of a new Session of Parliament in England were so closely copied, and so gravely presented on a small scale, that it was like looking at Westminster through the wrong end of a telescope. The Governor, as Her Majesty's representative, delivered what may be called the Speech from the Throne. He said what he had to say manfully and well. The military band outside the building struck up "God save the Queen" with great vigour before His Excellency had quite finished; the people shouted; the in's rubbed their hands; the out's shook their heads; the Government party said there never was such a good speech; the Opposition declared there never was such a bad one; the Speaker and members of the House of Assembly withdrew from the bar to say a great deal among themselves and do a little: and, in short, everything went on, and promised to go on, just as it does at home upon the like occasions.

This common attachment of the Dominion and provincial governments to the English parent (for even Quebec with its different antecedents has for many years looked to England for its inspiration in parliamentary matters) helps to simplify the study of the governments of the provinces. It has produced a striking similarity in Dominion and provincial political institutions and practices. A fairly accurate conception of many characteristics of provincial governments can thus be obtained by viewing them as adaptations of allied federal forms and constitutional customs. Moreover, the English attachment, aided by association with the Dominion and other provinces, has further tended to mould provincial governments into a fairly uniform type so that in essentials they look very much alike. A few differences may be found, but in most respects the provinces can be conveniently studied as one government rather than ten.

A substantial part of the government of the provinces has already been discussed. The general place of the provinces in the federation, their powers under the British North America Act, their financial difficulties, the system of provincial and local courts—all these have been noted in the preceding pages. The party organization in the provinces will be covered in the final chapter. The chief remaining features are discussed below.

PROVINCIAL CONSTITUTIONS

The provincial constitutions, like that of the Dominion, are of a varied composition. The British North America Act and provincial statutes furnish the legal framework; and this is added to, modified, and interpreted by custom, judicial decision, orders-in-council, rules of the legislature, etc. Unlike the Dominion, however, the provinces are given the power to amend their written constitutions, for Section 92 of the British North America Act gives to their legislatures the power to amend "notwithstanding anything in this Act, . . . the constitution of the province, except as regards the office of Lieutenant-Governor." A provincial legislature, for example, has in the past abolished its upper house or Legislative Council, increased the term of the existing legislature, and even, on one occasion, legislated some of its own members into seats in a new legislature without the necessity of running an election.

This sweeping legislative power, whether used for amending the constitution or for enacting ordinary statutes (there is no difference whatever in the statutory form of these two operations) is subject to certain restrictions, or possible restrictions:

1. It cannot be used to alter the distribution of power between the federation and the provinces.

2. It cannot, as already noted, alter the office of the Lieutenant-Governor, who is a Dominion official.

3. Provincial legislation under the terms of the British North America Act may be disallowed by the Governor-General-in-Council within one year of its receipt by the Dominion Government. This is a power which may be used to render inoperative and void any provincial act whatsoever and for any reason which may seem fitting to the Dominion Government. "Contrary to sound principles of legislation", "ultra vires", "unjust", "discriminatory", are some of the reasons which have been given in the past. A total of 112 provincial acts have been disallowed since Confederation. The use of this power is uncertain and sporadic, but it is still active and has been invoked a number of times in recent years.

4. Closely allied to the power of disallowance is Dominion action or inaction on provincial bills which may be "reserved" by the Lieutenant-Governor for the consideration and approval of the Dominion Government. Any provincial bill may be subjected to this treatment, and if the Governor-General-in-Council withholds its assent, the bill does not become law.

THE LIEUTENANT-GOVERNOR

The head of the provincial government is the Lieutenant-Governor, who is the representative of the Crown in the province. He is appointed by the Governor-General-in-Council for a five-year term, and as a Dominion officer is paid by the federal government. He may be removed "for cause assigned" by the Governor-General-in-Council.

The parallel between the Dominion and provincial governments is least reliable when applied to the Governor-General and the Lieutenant-Governor, for while the positions were not dissimilar in 1867, they have steadily diverged since that time. Each Governor was expected to perform a double function: first, as the agent or representative of the government which appointed him, and second, as the head of the government in the colony. But while the Governor-General has now become completely cut off from the British Government, the Lieutenant-Governor still remains an official of the Dominion and, as such, subject to its instructions. The Governor-General, moreover, has become with the years increasingly dependent on his Cabinet, but the Lieutenant-Governor has time and again asserted an independent authority in the government of the province.

The British North America Act gave to the Governor-General and to the Lieutenant-Governor respectively certain powers in regard to legislation. The Governor-General (or the Lieutenant-Governor) had the power to *withhold his assent* from any bill passed by the Canadian (or provincial) legislature, or to *reserve* it for the consideration of the British (or Canadian) Government, which could later approve it or allow it to remain inoperative. The Governor-General has never withheld his assent to a Canadian bill. The exercise of his power of reservation virtually ceased a decade or so after Confederation, and it has now been completely abandoned. The corresponding powers of the Lieutenant-Governor, on the other hand, are far from obsolete. Canadian history, even in recent years, has furnished frequent cases of reservation and occasional cases where assent has been refused. In some of these instances the Lieutenant-Governor has followed instructions from Ottawa; in others, he has acted on his own initiative.

Lieutenant-Governors have also occasionally asserted their right to disregard the advice of their Cabinets and to take independent action. A Lieutenant-Governor has at various times dismissed a Cabinet from office, refused a dissolution, compelled his Cabinet to appoint a Royal Commission of investigation, refused to sign an order-in-council recommended by his Cabinet, and rejected a recommendation by his Cabinet for an appointment. It is not possible here to discuss these incidents nor to inquire if they have had adequate justification. They provide, in any event, substantial evidence to show that the Lieutenant-Governor is more than a passive instrument in the hands of his Cabinet. The normal practice, of course, is that he acts under advice; but on occasion he has proved to be quite prepared to set his opinion against that of his constitutional advisers and on far more flimsy pretexts than any advanced by any Governor-General since Confederation.

THE CABINET

The Cabinet dominates the government of a province in much the same way and to the same extent as the federal Cabinet dominates the government of Canada. The Premier takes office on the invitation of the Lieutenant-Governor; he chooses the Cabinet; he is the leader of his party in the province, the leader of the majority in the Legislative Assembly, and the leader and outstanding figure in the Cabinet. All members of the Cabinet must have seats in the legislature, and the Cabinet is at all times responsible to the Assembly. There have been times in one or two provinces, however, when the legislature has wavered in its support of the usual strict rules of parliamentary responsibility, and at such times it has taken the position that the defeat of a Government measure would not necessitate the resignation of the Cabinet unless it were followed by a vote of non-confidence. On a few rare occasions also, Ministers have voted against bills introduced by other Ministers, a practice which clearly violates the generally accepted principle of Cabinet solidarity.

A Premier usually gives representation in the Cabinet to different areas and interests in the province. This custom combined with the wide diversity of administrative duties tends to produce a large Cabinet, especially in relation to the moderate size of the Assembly. In most provinces the Cabinet will include about ten Ministers, although in 1947 the Ontario and Quebec Cabinets were composed of sixteen and twenty-one members respectively. Ministers are in most instances heads of administrative departments, although Ministers without portfolio are not uncommon. The Quebec Cabinet mentioned above contained six without portfolio. In the smaller provinces Ministers are frequently placed in charge of more than one department.

THE DEPARTMENTS

The chief departments with some of their usual activities are given below. The distribution of departmental functions naturally varies with each province, although the main variations occur with a number of small matters which do not come definitely within the scope of one department more than another. It will be observed that most of the departmental activities affect the daily life of the average citizen much more closely than do those of the federal government.

1. *Agriculture.* This department has charge of a very wide variety of activities directly or indirectly associated with the encouragement and development of agriculture. Agricultural schools and colleges; research, and experimental farms and plots; farmers' societies; improvement of live-stock, field crops, soils, dairying, etc.; marketing schemes; weed and pest control; seed cleaning and spraying demonstrations; field extension work of all kinds; conservation; women's institutes—these are the more important undertakings of this department.

2. *Attorney-General.* This is the legal department of the government and, as such, it watches over the work of minor courts, sheriffs, registrars, prothonotaries, coroners, and other legal officers, and co-operates with them. It also recommends legal appointments. It enforces the law and prosecutes offenders under all Dominion laws, notably the Canada

Criminal Code, and all provincial laws, such as the Highways Act, and the Liquor Control Act. In some provinces it may issue liquor licences to hotels, and inspect premises.

3. *Education.* The name of this department clearly indicates its functions. It deals with the supervision and inspection of teaching and schools; health of school-children; curricula; normal school and summer courses; trade schools; vocational guidance; public libraries and archives; departmental publications; correspondence courses; radio broadcasting for educational purposes; and, indirectly, university education.

4. *Health.* This has charge of provincial hospitals, asylums, homes, sanitaria, etc.; regulation and inspection of similar private institutions; assistance to local hospitals; educational projects on dental health, maternal and child hygiene, etc.; industrial hygiene and occupational diseases; regulation and inspection of lumber, mining, and construction camps; research and testing laboratories; public health nursing; registration of nurses; sanitary engineering; psychiatric services; control of preventable diseases; and—in Saskatchewan —supervision of a municipal physician system.

5. *Highways.* This department has charge of the construction and maintenance of highways and bridges; the ploughing of snow on the main highways; the issuing of motor vehicle and drivers' licences, and the collection of the appropriate fees.

6. *Labour.* This department endeavours to promote fair dealing in labour matters and regulate by law and administration such matters as collective bargaining, the right to strike, union security, check-off, general labour practices, child and female labour, industrial standards, apprenticeship, hours of labour, factory conditions, etc. A substantial part of the work is frequently given to such independent bodies as a Workmen's Compensation Board, a Minimum Wages Board, and a Labour Relations Board. The depart-

ment also provides facilities for conciliation and arbitration, examines and certifies operating engineers, and inspects boilers.

7. *Lands and Forests.* This has the control of Crown lands and the general oversight of those privately owned. It buys, sells, and leases public lands; administers provincial parks and forests; maintains forest fire protective services; aids in municipal and private reforestation; conducts soil surveys, soil erosion studies, and insect pest research; and is responsible for publicity campaigns on conservation and allied problems.

8. *Mines.* This keeps all records of mineral production; conducts geological surveys; gives technical information and assistance to mining projects; formulates regulations for and inspects the operation of mines; investigates accidents and promotes safety measures and appliances; conducts examinations to determine the competence of miners and mine officials; and maintains assay offices.

9. *Municipal Affairs.* This department acts in an advisory and authorizing capacity to municipal bodies. It will approve proposed capital undertakings by a municipality; authorize the issue of municipal bonds; ensure that adequate "sinking funds" are set aside to pay off long-term loans; audit municipal accounts and compel the keeping of proper records; render various technical services to municipalities which cannot supply them; advise on town planning, assessment, budgeting, and all municipal problems.

10. *Provincial Secretary.* This tends to be an omnibus department in most provinces. It has charge of all communications between the province and other governments, and supervision over a large number of miscellaneous functions (which vary greatly from province to province) such as vital and other statistics; boards of parole; reformatories and industrial farms; motion picture censorship; supervision of insurance and other companies; water powers; issuing of

occupational licences; inspection of credit unions; and the government printing office.

11. *Provincial Treasurer.* This has general supervision of all expenditures and the collection of some of the revenue, although the latter will usually be derived from several departments and other sources. The subsidy from the Dominion is not raised, of course, by the province; a very large revenue comes also from the provincial liquor board; and succession duties, land taxes, and other levies such as fees and automobile licences may be more conveniently collected by other departments and paid over to the Treasurer. The department controls and supervises provincial loans, the debt of the province, and provincial and municipal sinking funds, and it advises all departments on financial matters. It also performs important auditing functions for the entire service, and is responsible for assembling all budgetary material and preparing the budget. In many provinces the Premier holds the office of Provincial Treasurer.

12. *Public Welfare.* This department supervises the administration of the greater part of the social services conducted either by the province alone or in association with the Dominion under "grants-in-aid". The major services are unemployment relief, old age pensions, mothers' allowances, child welfare, adoption, day nurseries, and homes for the aged. In a number of instances the department is assisted by a permanent board, some members of which hold no other government position.

13. *Public Works.* This department has the supervision, care, and maintenance of all provincial buildings—legislative and departmental buildings, Government House, normal schools, agricultural colleges, reformatories, hospitals, schools for the deaf and blind, etc.

Other departments or divisions are of minor importance in some provinces or occur in some and not in others, such as, telephones, co-operatives, industry, publicity, fisheries, development, game, and colonization. The provincial governments have experimented with public ownership, at times on a very large scale, notably in hydro-electric power, railways, telephones, and the sale of alcoholic liquor. For some of these enterprises and for many other administrative tasks provincial governments have often used boards and commissions to replace or to assist the regular departmental staff. Liquor boards, hydro-electric commissions, and public utility commissions are by far the most common of these.

THE CIVIL SERVICE

The provincial civil servants, like those of the Dominion, necessarily carry a very large and important part of the burden of government. They administer the provincial statutes; they draft the rules and regulations for the approval of the Lieutenant-Governor-in-Council; they advise their Minister; and in some departments they are the ones who must work out co-operative measures with Dominion civil servants who are engaged in allied fields of endeavour. The Minister, however, is rarely as dependent on his officials as is the political head of a Dominion department. The area which is covered is much more restricted, and the provincial Minister is able to exercise a greater and more direct influence in departmental decisions of all kinds. This close contact with administration is very pronounced in the smaller provinces, although even in the larger provinces the same tendency is found.

The civil service in all provinces was for many years filled by patronage, and reform has lagged almost a generation behind the Dominion. The inescapable demand for skilled and trained officials in many branches of provincial activity, however, has done more to improve the service than any statutory change, for in many positions party appointment is simply not able to supply the kind of personnel that the administration must have if it is to do its work properly. Thus while Ministers still continue to make most appointments and open competition is the exception, many of the civil servants actually obtain their position through ability and not by virtue of any claims they may have on the dominant political party.

THE LEGISLATURE

Although a number of the provinces began with a legislature of two chambers, Quebec is the only one which still retains an upper house. The Legislative Council of Quebec is composed of twenty-four members, appointed by the Lieutenant-Governor-in-Council for life. The Councillors have the same qualifications as Canadian senators and each represents a senatorial district. In 1947, two Councillors were, indeed, senators as well. The position and functions of the Legislative Council are substantially those of the Senate.

The Legislative Assembly is the popularly elected body in all provinces. Its membership varies from thirty in Prince Edward Island to ninety in Ontario and ninety-one in Quebec. While these numbers are small, they are sufficient to give adequate representation within the limited provincial area. The maximum term is five years, although a dissolution may occur at any time.

Each province has its own franchise, or rules which determine who shall be allowed to vote. In general, these rules are broad enough to enfranchise all adults, subject to a few special qualifications and disqualifications. The legislature of Prince Edward Island is unique in that one-half its members are called Councillors and are elected on a property franchise, while the other half are called Assemblymen and are elected by both property and non-property holders. No distinction whatever is drawn between these two kinds of members in the Legislative Assembly.

Single-member constituencies are the rule in all provinces except Prince Edward Island, where each constituency elects

LEGISLATIVE BUILDING, ST. JOHN'S

Marshall Studios Ltd.

PROVINCIAL BUILDING, CHARLOTTETOWN

P.E.I. Government

CITY FINANCE COMMITTEE IN SESSION, WINNIPEG

National Film Board

NATIONAL PARTY CONVENTION

Malak

a Councillor and an Assemblyman. Plural-member constituencies occur in certain other provinces under exceptional circumstances.

The difficulty already noted in federal elections, where winning candidates are often elected with less than an actual majority of votes, has been encountered also in the provinces. A possible remedy is to allow the voter in single-member districts to indicate a preference (voting 1, 2, 3, etc. for first, second, third, etc. choices) on his ballot. This vote by a system of the elimination of the lowest candidates and a transfer according to the alternative choices indicated on their ballots can be employed to ensure a majority for the winner.

Another remedy, known as proportional representation, uses a large constituency electing three or more members. Here a preferential vote combined with an elaborate system of transferred ballots (too complicated to describe here) will secure the representation of the majority and minority opinions in proportion to the size of the vote cast by each.

Manitoba and Alberta use these systems to elect members to the Legislative Assembly. The cities of Winnipeg, Edmonton, and Calgary have multi-member constituencies with proportional representation; and the other constituencies in these provinces, while electing only one member, use the preferential vote first described above.

Party distinctions are found in the provinces on the same lines as in national politics, and the party organization is the same for both.[1] Small and local parties are, however, far more common and more vigorous in provincial politics, for they tend to win their early victories in the province and move on from there to the wider federal field. The emergence of these minor parties and the consequent splitting of the vote makes it more difficult for any one party to obtain a majority of seats in the Assembly, and provincial coalitions have therefore become increasingly frequent in recent years. On

[1] See pp. 126-9.

the other hand, the small number of seats sometimes makes it possible for a very popular party to gain so sweeping a victory that the combined opposition representation is reduced to a mere two or three members, a condition which is not conducive to efficiency in the Assembly.

The small size of many provincial legislatures may on occasion render certain formalities and procedures of parliamentary government unwieldy and ill-adapted to the work to be done. In some instances they have been dropped or modified. In others, they have been retained, although the conduct of some of the parliamentary business has as a result assumed an air of unreality and undue formality which has tended to detract from its efficiency.

In two provinces representative government in the legislature may be supplemented by direct appeals to the people for a decision on special subjects One of these methods of appeal is known as the *referendum*, which provides for a specific issue to be submitted to a popular vote for approval or rejection. Another is the *initiative*, whereby any voter who is able to secure a certain number of names to a petition can propose a law and have it voted on by the people. Both the referendum and the initiative are available in Alberta and British Columbia, though the results in each instance are not effective until they are confirmed by subsequent action by the Assembly. The Assembly, however, is not supposed to have any alternative but to implement the expressed wishes of the people. In actual practice, very little use is made of this type of "direct" legislation.

In all provinces (and in the Dominion as well) the people have occasionally been consulted by *plebiscite* or direct vote on a particular issue. In these cases, however, the Assembly (or Parliament) has been free to treat the vote as nothing more than an expression of opinion, and it has been under no obligation to enforce the verdict by enacting legislation.

Another political expedient closely allied to the initiative and the referendum is the *recall*. This procedure is used to get an elected official out of office, either by popular vote or by action of a party authority. In certain of the western provinces some political parties have used an informal system whereby a member of the legislature may be forced to resign on the demand of the members of his party. Alberta, however, at one time provided by statute for the recall of members of the Assembly by means of a formal petition, signed by a large percentage of the voters in the constituency concerned, followed by a new election to fill the vacancy. After a few months the statute was repealed.

CHAPTER FOURTEEN

Municipal Government

MUNICIPAL government is usually regarded as one of the great entrenchments of democracy. The voter is here in much closer touch with those he elects than in government at higher levels. He knows them better, he can see and judge more readily the results of his choice and the services performed, and he is frequently more intimately affected by the acts and policies of the local governing bodies.

The British North America Act gives "municipal institutions" and matters of "a merely local or private nature" to the provincial legislature, so that all municipal bodies derive their powers from the provincial authority. These institutions are not at all the same in each province. Indeed, Prince Edward Island and Newfoundland have no separate municipal institutions except for a few urban and educational authorities. Even within a particular province municipal institutions will assume a variety of forms, depending primarily upon what they are expected to do and upon the density of population within the different local areas. In all but the Maritime Provinces (not including Newfoundland) there are, indeed, large sparsely populated areas where there are no municipal institutions at all; although, as they become settled, the provincial authority provides for the creation of local governing units.

Municipal governmental areas fall into two chief divisions: urban, which includes cities, towns, and villages; and rural, which includes units variously known as counties, municipalities, parishes, townships, rural districts, etc.

URBAN GOVERNMENTS

The form and powers of urban governments are usually given in provincial statutes of general application, but the larger cities may be the creation of special acts or charters. The members of the urban councils are often elected by wards, although election "at large" (that is, using the entire area as one voting district) is also common. The mayor, however, is usually elected at large, though occasionally he is chosen by the council. The term for mayor and council varies, but it is normally one or two years. All councils in all provinces exercise legislative powers by passing by-laws, authorizing expenditures, and imposing taxes. All use committees very freely; and where there is no board of control, these committees are responsible for the great bulk of the administration as well. In the large cities in Ontario the council becomes for the most part a legislative body, and executive functions are primarily vested in a small board of control[1] which is elected at large. The board, acting with the mayor, prepares estimates, recommends expenditures, supervises the departments, makes contracts, and performs various administrative functions.

RURAL GOVERNMENTS

The county, rural municipality, or rural district has approximately the same general type of government throughout Canada, although in Ontario and Quebec it is not immediately based on popular election but rests on smaller municipal governing bodies. In these two provinces the local municipalities (towns, townships, parishes, and villages) elect their own councils which perform certain designated functions; while the county council is composed of one or two representatives (mayor, or reeve and deputy reeves) from these local municipalities, and is made responsible for

[1] This is an optional arrangement also in British Columbia.

different functions. In the other provinces, however, the county council is the primary body and is direct'y elected, sometimes by sub-divisions, divisions, or parishes, sometimes over the whole area. In all provinces the warden or chief officer of the county council is elected by and from its own members.

The most common term for the county councils is one or two years. In some provinces (and not always in the same province) towns may be separated in their government from the county of which they form a part; in others, they share municipal functions with the county council.

These councils work both as a whole and through standing committees appointed for special purposes of administration, such as, finance, welfare, public works. The council appoints assessors, clerks, collectors, and other officials on a full- or part-time basis, although as these are statutory positions, the duties are specified and the officials are in these matters not subject to its direction. County as well as urban councils have the power to enact by-laws, levy taxes, and authorize expenditures.

SPECIAL GOVERNING BODIES

In addition to these urban and rural municipal bodies of general jurisdiction, there are other bodies which are designed to serve special purposes. By far the most important of these are the educational boards which are found in some form in every province. These are, as a rule, elected separately, and they are virtually independent of other municipal bodies. When separate denominational schools are maintained, some such isolation of educational boards is imperative. The board will usually allot and determine the amount of money to be spent; but the school tax rate is set and the tax is collected as a rule by the municipal authorities. The local expenses of education are always defrayed in part by the provincial government.

Parks, police, water supply, public health, public utilities, and other municipal enterprises and services are frequently entrusted to special bodies elected or appointed for the purpose, and these enjoy varying degrees of independence from the regular municipal government. They are much more common in urban than in rural areas.

PROVINCIAL-MUNICIPAL RELATIONS

The current problems of provincial-municipal relations are strikingly reminiscent of the difficulties which have arisen between the federal and provincial governments; for they spring primarily from expanding municipal functions and the insufficiency of municipal funds to meet the increased strain which has been placed on them. For many years past the municipalities, particularly the cities and towns, have been importuned to take over new responsibilities and to enlarge those already assumed, such as, road improvement, snow removal, libraries, lighting, garbage and sewage disposal, poor relief, fire protection, water supply, hospitals, and health services. In many of these instances the province has unloaded its worries on municipal shoulders. Though a large number of the new activities may have been desirable, and even necessary, they have all involved increased expenditure which the municipal governments were ill-equipped to bear. Approximately four-fifths of municipal revenue is derived from taxes on real property, which press heavily on the poorer areas and are nowhere elastic enough to form a satisfactory basis for a taxing system. The natural result is that municipal bodies have been extremely reluctant to take on any new functions, and some have been too parsimonious in discharging many of their existing responsibilities.

Closely connected with this situation has been the growing tendency of the provincial governments to intervene in municipal affairs. The avowed purpose has been to compel the municipalities to discharge their duties more efficiently; the depression of the nineteen-thirties, involving as it often did municipal financial embarrassments and defaults, presented the opportunity. The result is that the provincial governments have become much more exacting in their regulations regarding municipal indebtedness, borrowing powers, sinking funds, records, procedures, accounting systems, etc., as well as in standards of performance for various municipal services. There is no doubt that many of these regulatory measures were very badly needed; but some of the provincial authorities are apt to show insufficient concern for the maintenance of municipal autonomy.

Provincial-municipal affairs are at the moment in a state of flux, and the remedies which are most often considered suggest the Dominion-provincial problem at another level. One remedy is increased grants or grants-in-aid from the provincial treasury, for there seems little likelihood that the municipalities can raise more revenue in an already overloaded tax system. Another is a re-distribution of powers so that the province will take over some of the functions which the municipalities now discharge. Yet another is a possible combination of the above. The financial situation in most of the provinces, however, is such that little can be done to relieve the municipalities until the provinces and the Dominion achieve a permanent adjustment in their relations. When those become stabilized, the provinces should be in a position where they can pass on some of the benefits, directly or indirectly, to the municipal governments.

CHAPTER FIFTEEN

Political Parties

WHILE political parties in Canada are largely unrecognized and uncontrolled by law, the throb of their activity is felt throughout the whole body politic. To such a degree is this true that the removal of the party influence and initiative would transform the existing system of government and would probably lead to its speedy dissolution.

What are the functions of political parties? In the first place, they have the chief responsibility for arousing the interest and educating the democracy on political matters. They also provide the organization whereby public opinion is able to add power and effectiveness to suggestion and criticism. The fact, moreover, that party members are forced to participate with many others in a joint endeavour inevitably brings about many compromises and concessions, so that resulting policy will form the highest common factor on which their conflicting interests are able to unite. Again, parties sort out and stress the major issues and they reduce the number of candidates. The task of the voter is thereby greatly simplified, and he is able to make his choice on a few questions and a few representative people.

The usefulness of parties is by no means confined to the constituencies. The foregoing pages have repeatedly indicated the many ways in which parties enter into the work of the Cabinet and the Parliament, adding to the effectiveness of the proceedings and sharpening the responsibility of both those in power and those in opposition. The party system ensures also that there will always be an alternative government available whenever the old one retires; and as its leaders and policies are well known and are prepared in advance, the transition can be made with a minimum of friction, uncertainty, and delay. Thus, while it is true that parties beget many evils—corruption, selfish interests, patronage, short-sighted policies, and so forth—it is undeniable that the benefits greatly outweigh the disadvantages.

A two-party system will, moreover, give better results under cabinet government than a system which rests on a multiplicity of parties; although if the additional parties are small and one party has a working majority, the objections are not so serious. Firm leadership, a dependable majority in the House, reasonably stable tenure for the Government, vigorous and responsible criticism from the Opposition—these are the fundamentals of good government, and they are most likely to be produced under a two-party system. Third and fourth parties may appear from time to time and they will often exert a beneficial influence on the others; but over any lengthy period their absorption by the major parties or the absorption of one of the major parties by the newcomer will serve the best interests of cabinet government.

Canada has in practice consistently approved of the two-party system, for while minor parties have frequently arisen, none of them has yet been able seriously to challenge the dominance of the Liberals and Conservatives. The present Co-operative Commonwealth Federation party (hereafter called the C.C.F.) is the most serious rival the older parties have encountered since the rise of the Progressives over twenty-five years ago.

MAJOR PARTIES

The views and policies which have distinguished the two major parties are not easily enumerated, for they have frequently been changeable and inconsistent. The most reliable test has been their attitude on the tariff. The Liberal-Conservatives (now known as Progressive Conservatives) have always advocated protection while the Liberals have favoured—with some periods of inertia—a definitely lower tariff. On other matters the party characteristics have been little more than general tendencies, usually reliable, but occasionally subject to modification and even at times to virtual abandonment. For example, the Conservatives have always prided themselves on their warm desire to maintain the Imperial connection, while the Liberals have advocated more nationalistic policies and have been impatient of fetters on Canadian powers of self-government. Yet it was a Liberal Government which introduced the Imperial tariff preference in 1897; while a Conservative Government during and after the First World War insisted on the Canadian right to control her own external relations, and another Conservative Government secured the passage of the Statute of Westminster.

For many years the party attitude on Dominion-provincial relations was a reliable point of contrast. The Conservatives were strong federalists and the Liberals were no less emphatic in their insistence on the rights of the provinces. Events since the Second World War, however, have brought an amazing change. The Liberals have now become the advocates of greater centralization, concentration of taxing powers, and development of social reforms under national auspices, while the Conservatives have developed tender feelings for the rights of the provinces. The tests of public ownership and progressive social legislation are equally inconclusive. Conservative Governments placed the Dominion in the railway business on a national scale, nationalized the radio, and enacted the Bennett "new deal" legislation of 1935. The Liberals, for their part, introduced old age pensions, unemployment insurance, and family allowances, and in 1948 began to develop an ambitious public health programme.

In one practical respect the Liberals have presented a marked contrast to the Conservatives: they have been able for almost sixty years to secure the votes and to a large degree the confidence of the people of Quebec. Ever since 1891 Quebec has elected a majority of Liberals to the House of Commons, and frequently these majorities have been overwhelming. The leadership of Sir Wilfrid Laurier, the

Liberal concern for provincial rights, and the Conservative stand on conscription have been factors in producing this result; but equally significant has been the much greater tolerance shown by the Liberals elsewhere in Canada towards the views and ambitions of Quebec even when a large number of the party members have disagreed with them. This toleration was particularly evident on the conscription issue, which did more to weaken the political position of the Conservative party than any other single factor. In eight out of nine general elections from 1917 to 1949 the Conservatives carried only 19 seats in Quebec out of a possible total of 528. In the election of 1930 the party carried 24 seats, and with this help attained office. It is generally admitted that no party in Canada can hope for a majority in the Commons without substantial support from Quebec, and it is this support which was largely responsible for the long Liberal tenure of office after 1921 with but two breaks, one of a few months and the other of five years. The same generalization might be made, of course, concerning the indispensability of backing from Ontario. The difference is that the Ontario votes have been fluid, and consequently a moderate number of Ontario seats has not been beyond the reach of either party.

Parties in Canada must, indeed, obtain substantial support from at least two and probably three of the five regional areas into which Canada is divided—the Maritime Provinces, Quebec, Ontario, the Prairie Provinces, and British Columbia. From this follows the logical consequence that a party, should strive at all costs to reconcile the conflicting interests of a number of these areas. The greater its success in this endeavour, the more likely is it to attain office.

A Canadian party must therefore be founded on compromise. It must pick and choose. It must balance one interest against another. It must postpone decisions. Its policies must be based on those things which are generally acceptable and then be gradually enlarged when and where the occasion suggests. Party platforms are thus notoriously unsatisfactory documents. On the one hand, they are forced to straddle many national issues which are likely to arouse antagonisms, while on the other, they are induced to cast their net far enough to include a large number of clauses which are designed to make a purely sectional appeal. The successful leader must surmount the same kind of obstacles, and he is thus forced to temporize and compromise to avoid splitting his following. It is no accident that the three Prime Ministers with the longest terms in office—Macdonald, Laurier, and King—have all been conspicuous for their willingness to make concessions, their skill in avoiding awkward or hasty decisions, and their ability to bring together people of divergent interests and beliefs.

The need for glossing over differences which might split the party forces has tended to elevate the party leader at the expense of its wavering principles, for all areas and groups can unite on a person far more readily than on a common idea. The platform is therefore not as vital as its interpretation by the leader or the proposals which he may bring forward to implement some of the party policies. The platform, as Mr. Mackenzie King was fond of saying, is to be regarded as a chart which is drawn by the party to serve as a guide for its leader. His very delicate task is to determine the extent to which it can be implemented and whether the time is opportune for the party to do so.

MINOR PARTIES

Minor parties in Canadian history have rarely had more than a local or group appeal, and thus while they have frequently captured the governments of one or two provinces, their impact on the Dominion Parliament has usually been slight. The Progressive party which arose after the First World War was the most successful, for in addition to constituting or sharing in two provincial Governments, it elected in 1921 no less than sixty-five members to the House of Commons. It was, however, a farmers' party. To that it owed its rapid success, its very limited national appeal, and its short life in federal politics of about five or six years. The Social Credit party has been even more localized, its economic theories having little endorsement outside Alberta.

Quebec has given birth to more minor parties than all the rest of Canada combined. They spring from special conditions in that province, and usually derive their strength from an aggressive provincialism and racialism which may be combined with a suspicion of and even a hostility to the rest of Canada. The present Union Nationale, for example, is rooted in Quebec issues to such a degree that it has so far shown little desire to enter federal politics at all, although in its advocacy of home rule and its opposition to the Liberals it has found an eager sympathizer in the Conservative party in Ontario.

The Communist party, which calls itself Labour-Progressive, has made little progress except in one or two provinces where it has elected an occasional member to a provincial legislature.

The C.C.F. has made substantial progress since the Second World War, although its standing as a national party is still in some doubt. It has attained office in Saskatchewan, is the official opposition in several other provinces, and has an active, aggressive group in the House of Commons. It is frankly socialist, and tends to look to the British Labour party for its inspiration. It aims at the nationalization of many industries and a more strict regulation of private enterprise, and proposes a comprehensive programme of social reform. The C.C.F. has made a fairly successful appeal to labour over all Canada (except in Quebec) and to farmers in a number of provinces.

PARTY ORGANIZATION

The organization of the major Canadian parties is made to fit into the framework of the political institutions themselves, for the two are of necessity closely related to one another.

Party organization thus begins with the smallest unit at the bottom, the individual poll within the constituency; then comes the party association of the constituency, then the provincial association, and finally the national association with its headquarters at Ottawa. In Ontario, the exceptionally large area and population has made it desirable to interpose other party bodies between the constituency and the province, known as regional or district associations, each of which includes from ten to twenty-five constituencies. There are also women's and young people's associations throughout Canada which run parallel to the regular hierarchy and which are given special representation in it at the provincial and national levels.

All these associations hold annual and special meetings, and each chooses directly or indirectly its own executive officers. The meetings afford an opportunity to the members to discuss various matters concerning the party's welfare, although they tend to let their officers perform most of the work.

The ordinary party members are most active at a different kind of gathering—the convention, which meets whenever it becomes necessary to nominate a candidate or to elect a party leader. The constituency convention usually consists of delegates chosen from each poll organization, and its chief function is to nominate a party candidate for a provincial or Dominion election. The provincial convention, composed of representatives from each constituency association and some *ex-officio* delegates, chooses a provincial leader. The national convention, which must of necessity represent the varied interests and groups throughout the Dominion, may have a membership as high as 1,200 or 1,300. This membership is in part chosen by the constituencies, in part *ex-officio*, and sometimes these may be augmented by other methods as well. Both provincial and national conventions also perform a secondary function of drafting a party platform.

All these meetings and conventions are designed to increase the voting strength of the party and to give the members a sense of effective participation in the party policies and in the direction of the party activity. There is, in fact, a great deal of autonomy and independence throughout the organization, although members with official standing—the party executive and the legislative and Cabinet members—are apt to exercise a preponderant influence in the deliberations and decisions, especially at the provincial and national levels. The provincial convention has been an established institution for a generation. The two major parties combined have held only six national conventions in fifty years, but there is every reason to expect that it is now a permanent part of the organization of both parties. The Liberal National Convention in 1948 even took the unprecedented step of deciding that the Liberals would call a national convention once every four years, a decision that is an indication of the way in which American party practices tend to be adopted in Canada.

One of the most notable characteristics of Canadian parties has been this susceptibility to American influences, and in no respect is this more evident than in the provincial and national conventions. The purposes of the conventions are identical with those of their American prototypes: they are held to choose a leader and to formulate a platform. In both countries the names of candidates are placed before the convention in nominating speeches, and the voting proceeds in successive ballots until one candidate receives a majority. The use of temporary and permanent chairmen, the "key-note" speech delivered early in the proceedings, the appointment of convention committees, the passage of interminable resolutions, the intense excitement, the frantic music, the bargaining for votes, the hand-shaking and back-slapping, have all been copied in Canada enthusiastically and with little discrimination. The chief points of difference are that in the United States the candidates do not address the convention, and the voting is oral and polled through each delegation; whereas in Canada the candidates are expected to speak, and the voting is by means of an individual secret printed ballot. The conventions in both countries are open to one comprehensive objection: the difficulty if not the impossibility of a thousand or more delegates, working in a frenzied environment, to devote adequate care and deliberation to the delicate tasks of choosing a leader and of enunciating the principles on which the party proposes to contest the next election.

The C.C.F. organization resembles in many respects that of the major parties, but a few special characteristics may be mentioned. One notable difference which occurs in some provinces is that instead of the poll committee at the bottom, there is the C.C.F. "club", a little group of members, which is designed for study, propaganda, and energetic canvassing. Non-political organizations, such as trade unions, are allowed to affiliate with the party, and are given a collective membership. Representation of these clubs and affiliated bodies is apt to produce a somewhat complicated membership in the party conventions. The C.C.F. also prides itself upon having its members participate more actively than the major parties at all stages of the party organization. It therefore has annual provincial conventions and a biennial national convention; and the resolutions passed at these meetings are more numerous and more varied than at conventions of the major parties. The C.C.F. members are apt to be more outspoken and critical of the provincial and national party leaders, and the leaders themselves are chosen afresh at each convention. There is also a much more pronounced tendency for the rank and file and their officers to try to control the party members in the Dominion and provincial legislatures. It is questionable whether some of these practices are as valuable as they pretend to be, but the organization of the major parties is not so perfect that they can afford to be too critical of an endeavour to make party democracy a little more real and more genuinely helpful in the intricate business of government.

APPENDICES

A. The British North America Act, 1867.
B. The British North America Act, 1871.
C. The Parliament of Canada Act, 1875.
D. The British North America Act, 1886.
E. The British North America Act, 1915.
F. The British North America Act, 1940.
G. The British North America Act, 1946.
H. The British North America Act, 1949.

A. THE BRITISH NORTH AMERICA ACT, 1867

Brit. Statutes, 30 Victoria, Chapter 3.

An Act for the Union of Canada, Nova Scotia, and New Brunswick, and the Government thereof; and for Purposes connected therewith.

[*29th March, 1867.*]

WHEREAS the Provinces of Canada, Nova Scotia, and New Brunswick have expressed their Desire to be federally united into One Dominion under the Crown of the United Kingdom of Great Britain and Ireland, with a Constitution similar in Principle to that of the United Kingdom:

And whereas such a Union would conduce to the Welfare of the Provinces and promote the Interests of the British Empire:

And whereas on the Establishment of the Union by Authority of Parliament it is expedient, not only that the Constitution of the Legislative Authority in the Dominion be provided for, but also that the Nature of the Executive Government therein be declared:

And whereas it is expedient that Provision be made for the eventual admission into the Union of other Parts of British North America:

Be it therefore enacted and declared by the Queen's most Excellent Majesty, by and with the Advice and Consent of the Lords Spiritual and Temporal, and Commons, in this present Parliament assembled, and by the Authority of the same, as follows:

I. PRELIMINARY.

1. This Act may be cited as the British North America Act, 1867. *Short Title.*

2. The Provisions of this Act referring to Her Majesty the Queen extend also to the Heirs and Successors of Her Majesty, Kings and Queens of the United Kingdom of Great Britain and Ireland. *Application of Provisions referring to the Queen.*

II. Union.

Declaration of Union.

3. It shall be lawful for the Queen, by and with the Advice of Her Majesty's Most Honourable Privy Council, to declare by Proclamation that, on and after a Day therein appointed, not being more than Six Months after the passing of this Act, the Provinces of Canada, Nova Scotia, and New Brunswick shall form and be One Dominion under the Name of Canada; and on and after that Day those Three Provinces shall form and be One Dominion under that Name accordingly.

Construction of subsequent Provisions of Act.

4. The subsequent Provisions of this Act shall, unless it is otherwise expressed or implied, commence and have effect on and after the Union, that is to say, on and after the Day appointed for the Union taking effect in the Queen's Proclamation; and in the same Provisions, unless it is otherwise expressed or implied, the Name Canada shall be taken to mean Canada as constituted under this Act.

Four Provinces.

5. Canada shall be divided into Four Provinces, named Ontario, Quebec, Nova Scotia, and New Brunswick.

Provinces of Ontario and Quebec.

6. The Parts of the Province of Canada (as it exists at the passing of this Act) which formerly constituted respectively the Provinces of Upper Canada and Lower Canada shall be deemed to be severed, and shall form two separate Provinces. The Part which formerly constituted the Province of Upper Canada shall constitute the Province of Ontario; and the Part which formerly constituted the Province of Lower Canada shall constitute the Province of Quebec.

Provinces of Nova Scotia and New Brunswick.

7. The Provinces of Nova Scotia and New Brunswick shall have the same Limits as at the passing of this Act.

Decennial Census.

8. In the general Census of the Population of Canada which is hereby required to be taken in the Year One thousand eight hundred and seventy-one, and in every Tenth Year thereafter, the respective Populations of the Four Provinces shall be distinguished.

III. EXECUTIVE POWER.

9. The Executive Government and Authority of and over Canada is hereby declared to continue and be vested in the Queen.

<small>Declaration of Executive Power in the Queen.</small>

10. The Provisions of this Act referring to the Governor General extend and apply to the Governor General for the Time being of Canada, or other the Chief Executive Officer or Administrator for the Time being carrying on the Government of Canada on behalf and in the Name of the Queen, by whatever Title he is designated.

<small>Application of Provisions referring to Governor General.</small>

11. There shall be a Council to aid and advise in the Government of Canada, to be styled the Queen's Privy Council for Canada; and the Persons who are to be Members of that Council shall be from Time to Time chosen and summoned by the Governor General and sworn in as Privy Councillors, and Members thereof may be from Time to Time removed by the Governor General.

<small>Constitution of Privy Council for Canada.</small>

12. All Powers, Authorities, and Functions which under any Act of the Parliament of Great Britain, or of the Parliament of the United Kingdom of Great Britain and Ireland, or of the Legislature of Upper Canada, Lower Canada, Canada, Nova Scotia, or New Brunswick, are at the Union vested in or exerciseable by the respective Governors or Lieutenant-Governors of those Provinces, with the Advice, or with the Advice and Consent, of the respective Executive Councils thereof, or in conjunction with those Councils, or with any Number of Members thereof, or by those Governors or Lieutenant-Governors individually, shall, as far as the same continue in existence and capable of being exercised after the Union in relation to the Government of Canada, be vested in and exerciseable by the Governor General, with the Advice or with the Advice and Consent of or in conjunction with the Queen's Privy Council for Canada, or any Members thereof, or by the Governor General individually, as the Case requires, subject nevertheless (except with respect to such as exist under Acts of the Parliament of Great Britain or of the Parliament of the United Kingdom of

<small>All Powers under Acts to be exercised by Governor General with advice of Privy Council or alone.</small>

Great Britain and Ireland) to be abolished or altered by the Parliament of Canada.

<small>Application of Provisions referring to Governor General in Council.</small> **13.** The Provisions of this Act referring to the Governor General in Council shall be construed as referring to the Governor General acting by and with the Advice of the Queen's Privy Council for Canada.

<small>Power to Her Majesty to authorize Governor General to appoint Deputies.</small> **14.** It shall be lawful for the Queen, if Her Majesty thinks fit, to authorize the Governor General from Time to Time to appoint any Person or any Persons jointly or severally to be his Deputy or Deputies within any Part or Parts of Canada, and in that Capacity to exercise during the Pleasure of the Governor General such of the Powers, Authorities, and Functions of the Governor General as the Governor General deems it necessary or expedient to assign to him or them, subject to any Limitations or Directions expressed or given by the Queen; but the Appointment of such a Deputy or Deputies shall not affect the Exercise by the Governor General himself of any Power, Authority, or Function.

<small>Command of Armed Forces to continue to be vested in the Queen.</small> **15.** The Command-in-Chief of the Land and Naval Militia, and of all Naval and Military Forces, of and in Canada, is hereby declared to continue and be vested in the Queen.

<small>Seat of Government of Canada.</small> **16.** Until the Queen otherwise directs the Seat of Government of Canada shall be Ottawa.

IV. LEGISLATIVE POWER.

<small>Constitution of Parliament of Canada.</small> **17.** There shall be One Parliament for Canada, consisting of the Queen, an Upper House styled the Senate, and the House of Commons.

<small>Privileges, etc., of Houses.</small> *18. The Privileges, Immunities, and Powers to be held, enjoyed, and exercised by the Senate and by the House of Commons and by the Members thereof respectively shall be such as are from Time to Time defined by Act of the Parliament of Canada, but so that the same shall never exceed those at the passing of this Act held, enjoyed, and exercised by the Com-

*Repealed by 1875 Amendment, and a new Section substituted. See Appendix C.

mons House of Parliament of the United Kingdom of Great Britain and Ireland and by the Members thereof.

19. The Parliament of Canada shall be called together not later than Six Months after the Union.

First Session of the Parliament of Canada.

20. There shall be a Session of the Parliament of Canada once at least in every Year, so that Twelve Months shall not intervene between the last Sitting of the Parliament in one Session and its first Sitting in the next Session.

Yearly Session of the Parliament of Canada.

The Senate.

*21. The Senate shall, subject to the Provisions of this Act, consist of Seventy-two Members, who shall be styled Senators.

Number of Senators.

22. In relation to the Constitution of the Senate, Canada shall be deemed to consist of Three Divisions;

Representation of Provinces in Senate.

1. Ontario;
2. Quebec;
3. The Maritime Provinces, Nova Scotia and New Brunswick; which Three Divisions shall (subject to the Provisions of this Act) be equally represented in the Senate as follows: Ontario by Twenty-four Senators; Quebec by Twenty-four Senators; and the Maritime Provinces by Twenty-four Senators, Twelve thereof representing Nova Scotia, and Twelve thereof representing New Brunswick.

In the Case of Quebec each of the Twenty-four Senators representing that Province shall be appointed for One of the Twenty-four Electoral Divisions of Lower Canada specified in Schedule A. to Chapter One of the Consolidated Statutes of Canada.

23. The Qualification of a Senator shall be as follows:

Qualifications of Senator.

(1) He shall be of the full age of Thirty Years:

(2) He shall be either a Natural-born Subject of the Queen, or a Subject of the Queen naturalized by an Act of the Parliament of Great Britain, or of the Parliament of the

*Altered by 1915 Amendment. See Appendix E.

United Kingdom of Great Britain and Ireland, or of the Legislature of One of the Provinces of Upper Canada, Lower Canada, Canada, Nova Scotia, or New Brunswick, before the Union, or of the Parliament of Canada, after the Union:

(3) He shall be legally or equitably seised as of Freehold for his own Use and Benefit of Lands or Tenements held in free and common Socage, or seised or possessed for his own Use and Benefit of Lands or Tenements held in Franc-alleu or in Roture, within the Province for which he is appointed, of the Value of Four thousand Dollars, over and above all Rents, Dues, Debts, Charges, Mortgages, and Incumbrances due or payable out of or charged on or affecting the same:

(4) His Real and Personal Property shall be together worth Four thousand Dollars over and above his Debts and Liabilities:

(5) He shall be resident in the Province for which he is appointed:

(6) In the case of Quebec he shall have his Real Property Qualification in the Electoral Division for which he is appointed, or shall be resident in that Division.

Summons of Senator. **24.** The Governor General shall from Time to Time, in the Queen's Name, by Instrument under the Great Seal of Canada, summon qualified Persons to the Senate; and, subject to the Provisions of this Act, every Person so summoned shall become and be a Member of the Senate and a Senator.

Summons of First Body of Senators. **25.** Such Persons shall be first summoned to the Senate as the Queen by Warrant under Her Majesty's Royal Sign Manual thinks fit to approve, and their Names shall be inserted in the Queen's Proclamation of Union.

Addition of Senators in certain cases. *26. If at any Time on the Recommendation of the Governor General the Queen thinks fit to direct that Three or Six Members be added to the Senate, the Governor General may by Summons to Three or Six qualified Persons (as the Case may be),

*Altered by 1915 Amendment. See Appendix E.

representing equally the Three Divisions of Canada, add to the Senate accordingly.

27. In case of such Addition being at any Time made the Governor General shall not summon any Person to the Senate, except on a further like Direction by the Queen on the like Recommendation, until each of the Three Divisions of Canada is represented by Twenty-four Senators and no more. *Reduction of Senate to normal number.*

28. The Number of Senators shall not at any Time exceed Seventy-eight. *Maximum number of Senators.*

29. A Senator shall, subject to the Provisions of this Act, hold his Place in the Senate for Life. *Tenure of Place in Senate.*

30. A Senator may by Writing under his Hand addressed to the Governor General resign his Place in the Senate, and thereupon the same shall be vacant. *Resignation of Place in Senate.*

31. The Place of a Senator shall become vacant in any of the following Cases:— *Disqualification of Senators.*

(1) If for Two consecutive Sessions of the Parliament he fails to give his Attendance in the Senate:

(2) If he takes an Oath or makes a Declaration or Acknowledgment of Allegiance, Obedience, or Adherence to a Foreign Power, or does an Act whereby he becomes a Subject or Citizen, or entitled to the Rights or Privileges of a Subject or Citizen, of a Foreign Power:

(3) If he is adjudged Bankrupt or Insolvent, or applies for the Benefit of any Law relating to Insolvent Debtors, or becomes a public Defaulter:

(4) If he is attainted of Treason or convicted of Felony or of any infamous Crime:

(5) If he ceases to be qualified in respect of Property or of Residence; provided, that a Senator shall not be deemed to have ceased to be qualified in respect of Residence by reason only of his residing at the Seat of the Government of Canada while holding an Office under that Government requiring his Presence there.

140 Democratic Government in Canada

Summons on Vacancy in Senate.
32. When a Vacancy happens in the Senate by Resignation, Death, or otherwise, the Governor General shall by Summons to a fit and qualified Person fill the Vacancy.

Questions as to Qualifications and Vacancies in Senate.
33. If any Question arises respecting the Qualification of a Senator or a Vacancy in the Senate the same shall be heard and determined by the Senate.

Appointment of Speaker of Senate.
34. The Governor General may from Time to Time, by Instrument under the Great Seal of Canada, appoint a Senator to be Speaker of the Senate, and may remove him and appoint another in his Stead.

Quorum of Senate.
35. Until the Parliament of Canada otherwise provides, the Presence of at least Fifteen Senators, including the Speaker, shall be necessary to constitute a Meeting of the Senate for the Exercise of its Powers.

Voting in Senate.
36. Questions arising in the Senate shall be decided by a Majority of Voices, and the Speaker shall in all Cases have a Vote, and when the Voices are equal the Decision shall be deemed to be in the Negative.

The House of Commons.

Constitution of House of Commons in Canada.
37. The House of Commons shall, subject to the Provisions of this Act, consist of One hundred and eighty-one Members, of whom Eighty-two shall be elected for Ontario, Sixty-five for Quebec, Nineteen for Nova Scotia, and Fifteen for New Brunswick.

Summoning of House of Commons.
38. The Governor General shall from Time to Time, in the Queen's Name, by Instrument under the Great Seal of Canada, summon and call together the House of Commons.

Senators not to sit in House of Commons.
39. A Senator shall not be capable of being elected or of sitting or voting as a Member of the House of Commons.

Electoral districts of the four Provinces.
40. Until the Parliament of Canada otherwise provides, Ontario, Quebec, Nova Scotia, and New Brunswick shall, for the Purposes of the Election of Members to serve in the House of Commons, be divided into Electoral Districts as follows:—

1. Ontario.

Ontario shall be divided into the Counties, Ridings of Counties, Cities, Parts of Cities, and Towns enumerated in the First Schedule to this Act, each whereof shall be an Electoral District, each such District as numbered in that Schedule being entitled to return One Member.

2. Quebec.

Quebec shall be divided into Sixty-five Electoral Districts, composed of the Sixty-five Electoral Divisions into which Lower Canada is at the passing of this Act divided under Chapter Two of the Consolidated Statutes of Canada, Chapter Seventy-five of the Consolidated Statutes for Lower Canada, and the Act of the Province of Canada of the Twenty-third Year of the Queen, Chapter One, or any other Act amending the same in force at the Union, so that each such Electoral Division shall be for the Purposes of this Act an Electoral District entitled to return One Member.

3. Nova Scotia.

Each of the Eighteen Counties of Nova Scotia shall be an Electoral District. The County of Halifax shall be entitled to return Two Members, and each of the other Counties One Member.

4. New Brunswick.

Each of the Fourteen Counties into which New Brunswick is divided, including the City and County of St. John, shall be an Electoral District. The City of St. John shall also be a separate Electoral District. Each of those Fifteen Electoral Districts shall be entitled to return One Member.

41. Until the Parliament of Canada otherwise provides, all Laws in force in the several Provinces at the Union relative to the following Matters or any of them, namely,—the Qualifications and Disqualifications of Persons to be elected or to sit or vote as Members of the House of Assembly or Legislative Assembly in the several Provinces, the Voters at Elections of

Continuance of existing Election Laws until Parliament of Canada otherwise provides.

such Members, the Oaths to be taken by Voters, the Returning Officers, their Powers and Duties, the Proceedings at Elections, the Periods during which Elections may be continued, the Trial of Controverted Elections, and Proceedings incident thereto, the vacating of Seats of Members, and the Execution of new Writs in case of Seats vacated otherwise than by Dissolution,—shall respectively apply to Elections of Members to serve in the House of Commons for the same several Provinces.

Provided that, until the Parliament of Canada otherwise provides, at any Election for a Member of the House of Commons for the District of Algoma, in addition to Persons qualified by the Law of the Province of Canada to vote, every male British Subject, aged Twenty-one Years or upwards, being a Householder, shall have a Vote.

<small>Writs for first Election.</small> **42.** For the First Election of Members to serve in the House of Commons the Governor General shall cause Writs to be issued by such Person, in such Form, and addressed to such Returning Officers as he thinks fit.

The Person issuing Writs under this Section shall have the like Powers as are possessed at the Union by the Officers charged with the issuing of Writs for the Election of Members to serve in the respective House of Assembly or Legislative Assembly of the Province of Canada, Nova Scotia, or New Brunswick; and the Returning Officers to whom Writs are directed under this Section shall have the like Powers as are possessed at the Union by the Officers charged with the returning of Writs for the Election of Members to serve in the same respective House of Assembly or Legislative Assembly.

<small>As to casual Vacancies.</small> **43.** In case a Vacancy in the Representation in the House of Commons of any Electoral District happens before the Meeting of the Parliament, or after the Meeting of the Parliament before Provision is made by the Parliament in this Behalf, the Provisions of the last foregoing Section of this Act shall extend and apply to the issuing and returning of a Writ in respect of such Vacant District.

<small>As to Election of</small> **44.** The House of Commons on its first assembling after a

The British North America Act, 1867

General Election shall proceed with all practicable Speed to elect One of its Members to be Speaker.

Speaker of House of Commons.

45. In case of a Vacancy happening in the Office of Speaker by Death, Resignation, or otherwise, the House of Commons shall with all practicable Speed proceed to elect another of its Members to be Speaker.

As to filling up Vacancy in Office of Speaker.

46. The Speaker shall preside at all Meetings of the House of Commons.

Speaker to preside.

47. Until the Parliament of Canada otherwise provides, in case of the Absence for any Reason of the Speaker from the Chair of the House of Commons for a period of Forty-eight consecutive Hours, the House may elect another of its Members to act as Speaker, and the Member so elected shall during the Continuance of such Absence of the Speaker have and execute all the Powers, Privileges, and Duties of Speaker.

Provision in case of absence of Speaker.

48. The Presence of at least Twenty Members of the House of Commons shall be necessary to constitute a Meeting of the House for the Exercise of its Powers; and for that Purpose the Speaker shall be reckoned as a Member.

Quorum of House of Commons.

49. Questions arising in the House of Commons shall be decided by a Majority of Voices other than that of the Speaker, and when the Voices are equal, but not otherwise, the Speaker shall have a Vote.

Voting in House of Commons.

50. Every House of Commons shall continue for Five Years from the Day of the Return of the Writs for choosing the House (subject to be sooner dissolved by the Governor General), and no longer.

Duration of House of Commons.

*51. On the Completion of the Census in the Year One thousand eight hundred and seventy-one, and of each subsequent decennial Census, the Representation of the Four Provinces shall be readjusted by such Authority, in such Manner, and from such Time, as the Parliament of Canada from Time to Time provides, subject and according to the following Rules:—

Decennial Re-adjustment of Representation.

*Repealed by 1946 Amendment, and a new Section substituted. See Appendix G.

(1) Quebec shall have the fixed Number of Sixty-five Members:

(2) There shall be assigned to each of the other Provinces such a Number of Members as will bear the same Proportion to the Number of its Population (ascertained at such Census) as the Number Sixty-five bears to the Number of the Population of Quebec (so ascertained):

(3) In the Computation of the Number of Members for a Province a fractional Part not exceeding One Half the whole Number requisite for entitling the Province to a Member shall be disregarded; but a fractional Part exceeding One Half of that Number shall be equivalent to the whole Number:

(4) On any such Re-adjustment the Number of Members for a Province shall not be reduced unless the Proportion which the Number of the Population of the Province bore to the Number of the aggregate Population of Canada at the then last preceding Re-adjustment of the Number of Members for the Province is ascertained at the then latest Census to be diminished by One Twentieth Part or upwards:

(5) Such Re-adjustment shall not take effect until the Termination of the then existing Parliament.

*

Increase of number of House of Commons. **52.** The Number of Members of the House of Commons may be from Time to Time increased by the Parliament of Canada, provided the proportionate Representation of the Provinces prescribed by this Act is not thereby disturbed.

Money Votes; Royal Assent.

Appropriation and tax Bills. **53.** Bills for appropriating any Part of the Public Revenue, or for imposing any Tax or Impost, shall originate in the House of Commons.

Recommendation of money votes. **54.** It shall not be lawful for the House of Commons to adopt or pass any Vote, Resolution, Address, or Bill for the Appropriation of any Part of the Public Revenue, or of any Tax or

*New Section 51A added by 1915 Amendment. See Appendix E.

The British North America Act, 1867

Impost, to any Purpose that has not been first recommended to that House by Message of the Governor General in the Session in which such Vote, Resolution, Address, or Bill is proposed.

55. Where a Bill passed by the Houses of Parliament is presented to the Governor General for the Queen's Assent, he shall declare, according to his Discretion, but subject to the Provisions of this Act and to Her Majesty's Instructions, either that he assents thereto in the Queen's Name, or that he withholds the Queen's Assent, or that he reserves the Bill for the Signification of the Queen's Pleasure. Royal Assent to Bills, etc.

56. Where the Governor General assents to a Bill in the Queen's Name, he shall by the first convenient Opportunity send an authentic Copy of the Act to one of Her Majesty's Principal Secretaries of State, and if the Queen in Council within Two Years after Receipt thereof by the Secretary of State thinks fit to disallow the Act, such Disallowance (with a Certificate of the Secretary of State of the Day on which the Act was received by him) being signified by the Governor General, by Speech or Message to each of the Houses of the Parliament or by Proclamation, shall annul the Act from and after the Day of such Signification. Disallowance by order in Council of Act assented to by Governor General.

57. A Bill reserved for the Signification of the Queen's Pleasure shall not have any Force unless and until within Two Years from the Day on which it was presented to the Governor General for the Queen's Assent, the Governor General signifies, by Speech or Message to each of the Houses of the Parliament or by Proclamation, that it has received the Assent of the Queen in Council. Signification of Queen's pleasure on Bill reserved.

An Entry of every such Speech, Message, or Proclamation shall be made in the Journal of each House, and a Duplicate thereof duly attested shall be delivered to the proper Officer to be kept among the Records of Canada.

V. PROVINCIAL CONSTITUTIONS.
Executive Power.

Appointment of Lieutenant-Governors of Provinces.

58. For each Province there shall be an Officer, styled the Lieutenant-Governor, appointed by the Governor General in Council by Instrument under the Great Seal of Canada.

Tenure of office of Lieutenant-Governor.

59. A Lieutenant-Governor shall hold Office during the Pleasure of the Governor General; but any Lieutenant-Governor appointed after the Commencement of the First Session of the Parliament of Canada shall not be removable within Five Years from his Appointment, except for Cause assigned, which shall be communicated to him in Writing within One Month after the Order for his Removal is made, and shall be communicated by Message to the Senate and to the House of Commons within One Week thereafter if the Parliament is then sitting, and if not then within One Week after the Commencement of the next Session of the Parliament.

Salaries of Lieutenant-Governors.

60. The Salaries of the Lieutenant-Governors shall be fixed and provided by the Parliament of Canada.

Oaths, etc., of Lieutenant-Governor.

61. Every Lieutenant-Governor shall, before assuming the Duties of his Office, make and subscribe before the Governor General or some Person authorized by him, Oaths of Allegiance and Office similar to those taken by the Governor General.

Application of provisions referring to Lieutenant-Governor.

62. The Provisions of this Act referring to the Lieutenant-Governor extend and apply to the Lieutenant-Governor for the Time being of each Province or other the Chief Executive Officer or Administrator for the Time being carrying on the Government of the Province, by whatever Title he is designated.

Appointment of Executive Officers for Ontario and Quebec.

63. The Executive Council of Ontario and of Quebec shall be composed of such Persons as the Lieutenant-Governor from Time to Time thinks fit, and in the first instance of the following Officers, namely,—the Attorney-General, the Secretary and Registrar of the Province, the Treasurer of the Province, the Commissioner of Crown Lands, and the Commissioner of Agriculture and Public Works, with in Quebec, the Speaker of the Legislative Council and the Solicitor General.

The British North America Act, 1867

64. The Constitution of the Executive Authority in each of the Provinces of Nova Scotia and New Brunswick shall, subject to the Provisions of this Act, continue as it exists at the Union until altered under the Authority of this Act.

Executive Government of Nova Scotia and New Brunswick.

65. All Powers, Authorities, and Functions which under any Act of the Parliament of Great Britain, or of the Parliament of the United Kingdom of Great Britain and Ireland, or of the Legislature of Upper Canada, Lower Canada, or Canada, were or are before or at the Union vested in or exerciseable by the respective Governors or Lieutenant-Governors of those Provinces, with the Advice or with the Advice and Consent of the respective Executive Councils thereof, or in conjunction with those Councils, or with any Number of Members thereof, or by those Governors or Lieutenant-Governors individually, shall, as far as the same are capable of being exercised after the Union in relation to the Government of Ontario and Quebec respectively, be vested in and shall or may be exercised by the Lieutenant-Governor of Ontario and Quebec respectively, with the Advice or with the Advice and Consent of or in conjunction with the respective Executive Councils, or any Members thereof, or by the Lieutenant-Governor individually, as the Case requires, subject nevertheless (except with respect to such as exist under Acts of the Parliament of Great Britain, or of the Parliament of the United Kingdom of Great Britain and Ireland,) to be abolished or altered by the respective Legislatures of Ontario and Quebec.

Powers to be exercised by Lieutenant-Governor of Ontario or Quebec with advice or alone.

66. The Provisions of this Act referring to the Lieutenant-Governor in Council shall be construed as referring to the Lieutenant-Governor of the Province acting by and with the Advice of the Executive Council thereof.

Application of provisions referring to Lieutenant-Governor in Council.

67. The Governor General in Council may from Time to Time appoint an Administrator to execute the Office and Functions of Lieutenant-Governor during his Absence, Illness, or other Inability.

Administration in absence, etc., of Lieutenant-Governor.

68. Unless and until the Executive Government of any Province otherwise directs with respect to that Province, the

Seats of Provincial Governments.

Seats of Government of the Provinces shall be as follows, namely,—of Ontario, the City of Toronto; of Quebec, the City of Quebec; of Nova Scotia, the City of Halifax; and of New Brunswick, the City of Fredericton.

Legislative Power.

1. ONTARIO.

<small>Legislature for Ontario.</small> **69.** There shall be a Legislature for Ontario consisting of the Lieutenant-Governor and of One House, styled the Legislative Assembly of Ontario.

<small>Electoral districts.</small> **70.** The Legislative Assembly of Ontario shall be composed of Eighty-two Members, to be elected to represent the Eighty-two Electoral Districts set forth in the First Schedule to this Act.

2. QUEBEC.

<small>Legislature for Quebec.</small> **71.** There shall be a Legislature for Quebec consisting of the Lieutenant-Governor and of Two Houses, styled the Legislative Council of Quebec and the Legislative Assembly of Quebec.

<small>Constitution of Legislative Council.</small> **72.** The Legislative Council of Quebec shall be composed of Twenty-four Members, to be appointed by the Lieutenant-Governor, in the Queen's Name, by Instrument under the Great Seal of Quebec, one being appointed to represent each of the Twenty-four Electoral Divisions of Lower Canada in this Act referred to, and each holding Office for the Term of his Life, unless the Legislature of Quebec otherwise provides under the Provisions of this Act.

<small>Qualification of Legislative Councillors.</small> **73.** The Qualifications of the Legislative Councillors of Quebec shall be the same as those of the Senators for Quebec.

<small>Resignation, Disqualification, etc.</small> **74.** The Place of a Legislative Councillor of Quebec shall become vacant in the Cases, *mutatis mutandis,* in which the Place of Senator becomes vacant.

<small>Vacancies.</small> **75.** When a Vacancy happens in the Legislative Council of Quebec by Resignation, Death, or otherwise, the Lieutenant-Governor, in the Queen's Name, by Instrument under the Great

Seal of Quebec, shall appoint a fit and qualified Person to fill the Vacancy.

76. If any Question arises respecting the Qualification of a Legislative Councillor of Quebec, or a Vacancy in the Legislative Council of Quebec, the same shall be heard and determined by the Legislative Council.

Questions as to Vacancies, etc.

77. The Lieutenant-Governor may from Time to Time, by Instrument under the Great Seal of Quebec, appoint a Member of the Legislative Council of Quebec to be Speaker thereof, and may remove him and appoint another in his stead.

Speaker of Legislative Council.

78. Until the Legislature of Quebec otherwise provides, the Presence of at least Ten Members of the Legislative Council, including the Speaker, shall be necessary to constitute a Meeting for the Exercise of its Powers.

Quorum of Legislative Council.

79. Questions arising in the Legislative Council of Quebec shall be decided by a Majority of Voices, and the Speaker shall in all Cases have a Vote, and when the Voices are equal the Decision shall be deemed to be in the negative.

Voting in Legislative Council.

80. The Legislative Assembly of Quebec shall be composed of Sixty-five Members, to be elected to represent the Sixty-five Electoral Divisions or Districts of Lower Canada in this Act referred to, subject to Alteration thereof by the Legislature of Quebec: Provided that it shall not be lawful to present to the Lieutenant-Governor of Quebec for Assent any Bill for altering the Limits of any of the Electoral Divisions or Districts mentioned in the Second Schedule to this Act, unless the Second and Third Readings of such Bill have been passed in the Legislative Assembly with the Concurrence of the Majority of the Members representing all those Electoral Divisions or Districts, and the Assent shall not be given to such Bill unless an Address has been presented by the Legislative Assembly to the Lieutenant Governor stating that it has been so passed.

Constitution of Legislative Assembly of Quebec.

3. Ontario and Quebec.

81. The Legislatures of Ontario and Quebec respectively

First Session of Legislatures

shall be called together not later than Six Months after the Union.

Summoning of Legislative Assemblies.
82. The Lieutenant-Governor of Ontario and of Quebec shall from Time to Time, in the Queen's Name, by Instrument under the Great Seal of the Province, summon and call together the Legislative Assembly of the Province.

Restriction on election of holders of offices.
83. Until the Legislature of Ontario or of Quebec otherwise provides, a Person accepting or holding in Ontario or in Quebec any Office, Commission, or Employment, permanent or temporary, at the Nomination of the Lieutenant-Governor, to which an annual Salary, or any Fee, Allowance, Emolument, or profit of any Kind or Amount whatever from the Province is attached, shall not be eligible as a Member of the Legislative Assembly of the respective Province, nor shall he sit or vote as such; but nothing in this Section shall make ineligible any Person being a Member of the Executive Council of the respective Province, or holding any of the following Offices, that is to say, the Offices of Attorney-General, Secretary and Registrar of the Province, Treasurer of the Province, Commissioner of Crown Lands, and Commissioner of Agriculture and Public Works, and in Quebec Solicitor General, or shall disqualify him to sit or vote in the House for which he is elected, provided he is elected while holding such Office.

Continuance of existing election Laws.
84. Until the Legislatures of Ontario and Quebec respectively otherwise provide, all Laws which at the Union are in force in those Provinces respectively, relative to the following Matters, or any of them, namely,—the Qualifications and Disqualifications of Persons to be elected or to sit or vote as Members of the Assembly of Canada, the Qualifications or Disqualifications of Voters, the Oaths to be taken by Voters, the Returning Officers, their Powers and Duties, the Proceedings at Elections, the Periods during which such Elections may be continued, and the Trial of controverted Elections and the Proceedings incident thereto, the vacating of the Seats of Members and the issuing and Execution of new Writs in case of Seats vacated otherwise than by Dissolution,—shall respectively

apply to Elections of Members to serve in the respective Legislative Assemblies of Ontario and Quebec.

Provided that until the Legislature of Ontario otherwise provides, at any Election for a Member of the Legislative Assembly of Ontario for the District of Algoma, in addition to Persons qualified by the Law of the Province of Canada to vote, every male British Subject, aged Twenty-one Years or upwards, being a Householder, shall have a Vote.

85. Every Legislative Assembly of Ontario and every Legislative Assembly of Quebec shall continue for Four Years from the Day of the Return of the Writs for choosing the same (subject nevertheless to either the Legislative Assembly of Ontario or the Legislative Assembly of Quebec being sooner dissolved by the Lieutenant-Governor of the Province), and no longer. Duration of Legislative Assemblies.

86. There shall be a session of the Legislature of Ontario and of that of Quebec once at least in every Year, so that Twelve Months shall not intervene between the last Sitting of the Legislature in each Province in one Session and its first Sitting in the next Session. Yearly Session of Legislature.

87. The following Provisions of this Act respecting the House of Commons of Canada shall extend and apply to the Legislative Assemblies of Ontario and Quebec, that is to say,—the Provisions relating to the Election of a Speaker originally and on Vacancies, the Duties of the Speaker, the absence of the Speaker, the Quorum, and the Mode of voting, as if those Provisions were here re-enacted and made applicable in Terms to each such Legislative Assembly. Speaker, Quorum, etc.

4. Nova Scotia and New Brunswick.

88. The Constitution of the Legislature of each of the Provinces of Nova Scotia and New Brunswick shall, subject to the Provisions of this Act, continue as it exists at the Union until altered under the Authority of this Act; and the House of Assembly of New Brunswick existing at the passage of this Act shall, unless sooner dissolved, continue for the Period for which it was elected. Constitutions of Legislatures of Nova Scotia and New Brunswick.

5. ONTARIO, QUEBEC, AND NOVA SCOTIA.

First Elections. **89.** Each of the Lieutenant-Governors of Ontario, Quebec and Nova Scotia shall cause Writs to be issued for the First Election of Members of the Legislative Assembly thereof in such Form and by such Person as he thinks fit, and at such Time and addressed to such Returning Officer as the Governor General directs, and so that the First Election of a Member of the Assembly for any Electoral District or any Subdivision thereof shall be held at the same Time and at the same Places as the Election for a Member to serve in the House of Commons of Canada for that Electoral District.

6. THE FOUR PROVINCES.

Application to Legislatures of provisions respecting money votes, etc. **90.** The following Provisions of this Act respecting the Parliament of Canada, namely,—the Provisions relating to Appropriation and Tax Bills, the Recommendation of Money Votes, the Assent to Bills, the Disallowance of Acts, and the Signification of Pleasure on Bills reserved,—shall extend and apply to the Legislatures of the several Provinces as if those Provisions were here re-enacted and made applicable in Terms to the respective Provinces and the Legislatures thereof, with the Substitution of the Lieutenant-Governor of the Province for the Governor General, of the Governor General for the Queen and for a Secretary of State, of One Year for Two Years, and of the Province for Canada.

VI. DISTRIBUTION OF LEGISLATIVE POWERS.

Powers of the Parliament.

Legislative Authority of Parliament of Canada. **91.** It shall be lawful for the Queen by and with the Advice and Consent of the Senate and House of Commons, to make Laws for the Peace, Order, and good Government of Canada, in relation to all Matters not coming within the Classes of Subjects by this Act assigned exclusively to the Legislatures of the Provinces; and for greater Certainty, but not so as to restrict the Generality of the foregoing Terms of this Section, it is hereby declared that (notwithstanding anything in this Act) the

The British North America Act, 1867

exclusive Legislative Authority of the Parliament of Canada extends to all Matters coming within the Classes of Subjects next hereinafter enumerated; that is to say,—

1. The Public Debt and Property.
2. The Regulation of Trade and Commerce.

*

3. The raising of Money by any Mode or System of Taxation.
4. The borrowing of Money on the Public Credit.
5. Postal Service.
6. The Census and Statistics.
7. Militia, Military and Naval Service, and Defence.
8. The fixing of and providing for the Salaries and Allowances of Civil and other Officers of the Government of Canada.
9. Beacons, Buoys, Lighthouses, and Sable Island.
10. Navigation and Shipping.
11. Quarantine and the Establishment and Maintenance of Marine Hospitals.
12. Sea Coast and Inland Fisheries.
13. Ferries between a Province and any British or Foreign Country or between Two Provinces.
14. Currency and Coinage.
15. Banking, Incorporation of Banks, and the Issue of Paper Money.
16. Savings Banks.
17. Weights and Measures.
18. Bills of Exchange and Promissory Notes.
19. Interest.
20. Legal Tender.
21. Bankruptcy and Insolvency.
22. Patents of Invention and Discovery.
23. Copyrights.
24. Indians, and Lands reserved for the Indians.
25. Naturalization and Aliens.
26. Marriage and Divorce.
27. The Criminal Law, except the Constitution of Courts of Criminal Jurisdiction, but including the Procedure in Criminal Matters.

*New Sub-section 2A added by 1940 Amendment. See Appendix F.

28. The Establishment, Maintenance, and Management of Penitentiaries.
29. Such Classes of Subjects as are expressly excepted in the Enumeration of the Classes of Subjects by this Act assigned exclusively to the Legislatures of the Provinces.

And any Matter coming within any of the Classes of Subjects enumerated in this Section shall not be deemed to come within the Class of Matters of a local or private Nature comprised in the Enumeration of the Classes of Subjects by this Act assigned exclusively to the Legislatures of the Provinces.

Exclusive Powers of Provincial Legislatures.

<small>Subjects of exclusive Provincial Legislation.</small> **92.** In each Province the Legislature may exclusively make Laws in relation to Matters coming within the Classes of Subjects next hereinafter enumerated, that is to say,—

1. The Amendment from Time to Time, notwithstanding anything in this Act, of the Constitution of the Province, except as regards the Office of Lieutenant-Governor.
2. Direct Taxation within the Province in order to the Raising of a Revenue for Provincial Purposes.
3. The borrowing of Money on the sole Credit of the Province.
4. The Establishment and Tenure of Provincial Offices and the Appointment and Payment of Provincial Officers.
5. The Management and Sale of the Public Lands belonging to the Province and of the Timber and Wood thereon.
6. The Establishment, Maintenance, and Management of Public and Reformatory Prisons in and for the Province.
7. The Establishment, Maintenance, and Management of Hospitals, Asylums, Charities, and Eleemosynary Institutions in and for the Province, other than Marine Hospitals.
8. Municipal Institutions in the Province.
9. Shop, Saloon, Tavern, Auctioneer, and other Licenses in order to the raising of a Revenue for Provincial, Local, or Municipal Purposes.
10. Local Works and Undertakings other than such as are

of the following Classes:—

(*a*) Lines of Steam or other Ships, Railways, Canals, Telegraphs, and other Works and Undertakings connecting the Province with any other or others of the Provinces, or extending beyond the Limits of the Province:

(*b*) Lines of Steam Ships between the Province and any British or Foreign Country:

(*c*) Such Works as, although wholly situate within the Province, are before or after their Execution declared by the Parliament of Canada to be for the general Advantage of Canada or for the Advantage of Two or more of the Provinces.

11. The Incorporation of Companies with Provincial Objects.
12. The Solemnization of Marriage in the Province.
13. Property and Civil Rights in the Province.
14. The Administration of Justice in the Province, including the Constitution, Maintenance, and Organization of Provincial Courts, both of Civil and of Criminal Jurisdiction, and including Procedure in Civil Matters in those Courts.
15. The Imposition of Punishment by Fine, Penalty, or Imprisonment for enforcing any Law of the Province made in relation to any Matter coming within any of the Classes of Subjects enumerated in this Section.
16. Generally all Matters of a merely local or private Nature in the Province.

Education.

93. In and for each Province the Legislature may exclusively make Laws in relation to Education, subject and according to the following Provisions:—

Legislation respecting Education.

1. Nothing in any such law shall prejudicially affect any Right or Privilege with respect to Denominational Schools which any Class of Persons have by Law in the Province at the Union:
2. All the Powers, Privileges, and Duties at the Union by Law conferred and imposed in Upper Canada on the Separate Schools and School Trustees of the Queen's Roman Catholic Subjects shall be and the same are hereby

extended to the Dissentient Schools of the Queen's Protestant and Roman Catholic Subjects in Quebec:

3. Where in any Province a System of Separate or Dissentient Schools exists by Law at the Union or is thereafter established by the Legislature of the Province, an Appeal shall lie to the Governor General in Council from any Act or Decision of any Provincial Authority affecting any Right or Privilege of the Protestant or Roman Catholic Minority of the Queen's Subjects in relation to Education:

4. In case any such Provincial Law as from Time to Time seems to the Governor General in Council requisite for the due Execution of the Provisions of this Section is not made, or in case any Decision of the Governor General in Council on any Appeal under this Section is not duly executed by the proper Provincial Authority in that Behalf, then and in every such Case, and as far only as the Circumstances of each Case require, the Parliament of Canada may make remedial Laws for the due Execution of the Provisions of this Section and of any Decision of the Governor General in Council under this Section.

Uniformity of Laws in Ontario, Nova Scotia, and New Brunswick.

Legislation for uniformity of Laws in three Provinces. **94.** Notwithstanding anything in this Act, the Parliament of Canada may make Provision for the Uniformity of all or any of the Laws relative to Property and Civil Rights in Ontario, Nova Scotia, and New Brunswick, and of the Procedure of all or any of the Courts in those Three Provinces, and from and after the passing of any Act in that Behalf the Power of the Parliament of Canada to make Laws in relation to any Matter comprised in any such Act shall, notwithstanding anything in this Act, be unrestricted; but any Act of the Parliament of Canada making Provision for such Uniformity shall not have effect in any Province unless and until it is adopted and enacted as Law by the Legislature thereof.

The British North America Act, 1867

Agriculture and Immigration.

95. In each Province the Legislature may make Laws in relation to Agriculture in the Province, and to Immigration into the Province; and it is hereby declared that the Parliament of Canada may from Time to Time make Laws in relation to Agriculture in all or any of the Provinces, and to Immigration into all or any of the Provinces; and any Law of the Legislature of a Province relative to Agriculture or to Immigration shall have effect in and for the Province as long and as far only as it is not repugnant to any Act of the Parliament of Canada. *Concurrent powers of Legislation respecting Agriculture, etc.*

VII. JUDICATURE.

96. The Governor General shall appoint the Judges of the Superior, District, and County Courts in each Province, except those of the Courts of Probate in Nova Scotia and New Brunswick. *Appointment of Judges.*

97. Until the Laws relative to Property and Civil Rights in Ontario, Nova Scotia, and New Brunswick, and the Procedure of the Courts in those Provinces, are made uniform, the Judges of the Courts of those Provinces appointed by the Governor General shall be selected from the respective Bars of those Provinces. *Selection of Judges in Ontario, etc.*

98. The Judges of the Courts of Quebec shall be selected from the Bar of that Province. *Selection of Judges in Quebec.*

99. The Judges of the Superior Courts shall hold office during good Behaviour, but shall be removable by the Governor General on Address of the Senate and House of Commons. *Tenure of office of Judges of Superior Courts.*

100. The Salaries, Allowances, and Pensions of the Judges of the Superior, District, and County Courts (except the Courts of Probate in Nova Scotia and New Brunswick), and of the Admiralty Courts in Cases where the Judges thereof are for the Time being paid by Salary, shall be fixed and provided by the Parliament of Canada. *Salaries, etc., of Judges.*

101. The Parliament of Canada may, notwithstanding anything in this Act, from Time to Time, provide for the Consti- *General Court of Appeal, etc.*

tution, Maintenance, and Organization of a General Court of Appeal for Canada, and for the Establishment of any additional Courts for the better Administration of the Laws of Canada.

VIII. REVENUES; DEBTS; ASSETS; TAXATION.

<small>Creation of Consolidated revenue fund.</small>

102. All Duties and Revenues over which the respective Legislatures of Canada, Nova Scotia, and New Brunswick before and at the Union had and have Power of Appropriation, except such portions thereof as are by this Act reserved to the respective Legislatures of the Provinces, or are raised by them in accordance with the special Powers conferred on them by this Act, shall form One Consolidated Revenue Fund, to be appropriated for the Public Service of Canada in the Manner and subject to the Charges in this Act provided.

<small>Expenses of Collection, etc.</small>

103. The Consolidated Revenue Fund of Canada shall be permanently charged with the Costs, Charges, and Expenses incident to the Collection, Management, and Receipt thereof, and the same shall form the first Charge thereon, subject to be reviewed and audited in such Manner as shall be ordered by the Governor General in Council until the Parliament otherwise provides.

<small>Interest of Provincial public debts.</small>

104. The annual Interest of the Public Debts of the several Provinces of Canada, Nova Scotia, and New Brunswick at the Union shall form the Second Charge on the Consolidated Revenue Fund of Canada.

<small>Salary of Governor General.</small>

105. Unless altered by the Parliament of Canada, the salary of the Governor General shall be Ten thousand Pounds Sterling Money of the United Kingdom of Great Britain and Ireland, payable out of the Consolidated Revenue Fund of Canada, and the same shall form the Third Charge thereon.

<small>Appropriation from time to time.</small>

106. Subject to the several Payments by this Act charged on the Consolidated Revenue Fund of Canada, the same shall be appropriated by the Parliament of Canada for the Public Service.

<small>Transfer of stocks, etc.</small>

107. All Stocks, Cash, Banker's Balances, and Securities

The British North America Act, 1867

for Money belonging to each Province at the time of the Union, except as in this Act mentioned, shall be the Property of Canada, and shall be taken in Reduction of the amount of the respective Debts of the Provinces at the Union.

108. The Public Works and Property of each Province, enumerated in the Third Schedule to this Act, shall be the Property of Canada. *Transfer of property in schedule.*

109. All Lands, Mines, Minerals, and Royalties belonging to the several Provinces of Canada, Nova Scotia, and New Brunswick at the Union, and all Sums then due or payable for such Lands, Mines, Minerals, or Royalties, shall belong to the several Provinces of Ontario, Quebec, Nova Scotia, and New Brunswick in which the same are situate or arise, subject to any Trusts existing in respect thereof, and to any Interest other than that of the Province in the same. *Property in Lands, Mines, etc.*

110. All Assets connected with such Portions of the Public Debt of each Province as are assumed by that Province shall belong to that Province. *Assets connected with Provincial debts.*

111. Canada shall be liable for the Debts and Liabilities of each Province existing at the Union. *Canada to be liable for Provincial debts.*

112. Ontario and Quebec conjointly shall be liable to Canada for the amount (if any) by which the Debt of the Province of Canada exceeds at the Union Sixty-two million five hundred thousand dollars, and shall be charged with Interest at the Rate of Five per Centum per Annum thereon. *Debts of Ontario and Quebec.*

113. The Assets enumerated in the Fourth Schedule to this Act belonging at the Union to the Province of Canada shall be the Property of Ontario and Quebec conjointly. *Assets of Ontario and Quebec.*

114. Nova Scotia shall be liable to Canada for the Amount (if any) by which its Public Debt exceeds at the Union Eight million Dollars, and shall be charged with Interest at the Rate of Five per Centum per Annum thereon. *Debt of Nova Scotia.*

115. New Brunswick shall be liable to Canada for the Amount (if any) by which its Public Debt exceeds at the Union Seven *Debt of New Brunswick.*

million Dollars, and shall be charged with Interest at the Rate of Five per Centum per Annum thereon.

Payment of interest to Nova Scotia and New Brunswick. **116.** In case the Public Debts of Nova Scotia and New Brunswick do not at the Union amount to Eight million and Seven million Dollars respectively, they shall respectively receive by half-yearly Payments in advance from the Government of Canada Interest at Five per Centum per Annum on the Difference between the actual Amounts of their respective Debts and such stipulated Amounts.

Provincial public property. **117.** The several Provinces shall retain all their respective Public Property not otherwise disposed of in this Act, subject to the Right of Canada to assume any Lands or Public Property required for Fortifications or for the Defence of the Country.

Grants to Provinces. ***118.** The following Sums shall be paid yearly by Canada to the several Provinces for the Support of their Governments and Legislatures:

	Dollars.
Ontario	Eighty thousand.
Quebec	Seventy thousand.
Nova Scotia	Sixty thousand.
New Brunswick	Fifty thousand.

Two hundred and sixty thousand; and an annual Grant in aid of each Province shall be made, equal to Eighty Cents per Head of the Population as ascertained by the Census of One thousand eight hundred and sixty-one, and in the Case of Nova Scotia and New Brunswick, by each subsequent Decennial Census until the Population of each of those two Provinces amounts to Four hundred thousand Souls, at which Rate such Grant shall thereafter remain. Such Grants shall be in full Settlement of all future Demands on Canada, and shall be paid half-yearly in advance to each Province; but the Government of Canada shall deduct from such Grants, as against any Province, all Sums chargeable as Interest on the Public Debt of that Province in excess of the several Amounts stipulated in this Act.

*Altered by the 1907 Amendment, supra, pp. 121-2, 140.

119. New Brunswick shall receive by half-yearly Payments in advance from Canada for the Period of Ten years from the Union an additional Allowance of Sixty-three thousand Dollars per Annum; but as long as the Public Debt of that Province remains under Seven million Dollars, a Deduction equal to the Interest at Five per Centum per Annum on such Deficiency shall be made from that Allowance of Sixty-three thousand Dollars.

Further grant to New Brunswick.

120. All Payments to be made under this Act, or in discharge of Liabilities created under any Act of the Provinces of Canada, Nova Scotia, and New Brunswick respectively, and assumed by Canada, shall, until the Parliament of Canada otherwise directs, be made in such Form and Manner as may from Time to Time be ordered by the Governor General in Council.

Form of payments.

121. All Articles of the Growth, Produce, or Manufacture of any one of the Provinces shall, from and after the Union, be admitted free into each of the other Provinces.

Canadian manufactures, etc.

122. The Customs and Excise Laws of each Province shall, subject to the Provisions of this Act, continue in force until altered by the Parliament of Canada.

Continuance of customs and excise laws.

123. Where Customs Duties are, at the Union, leviable on any Goods, Wares, or Merchandises in any Two Provinces, those Goods, Wares, and Merchandises may, from and after the Union, be imported from one of those Provinces into the other of them on Proof of Payment of the Customs Duty leviable thereon in the Province of Exportation, and on Payment of such further Amount (if any) of Customs Duty as is leviable thereon in the Province of Importation.

Exportation and Importation as between two Provinces.

124. Nothing in this Act shall affect the Right of New Brunswick to levy the Lumber Dues provided in Chapter Fifteen of Title Three of the Revised Statutes of New Brunswick, or in any Act amending that Act before or after the Union, and not increasing the Amount of such Dues; but the Lumber of any of the Provinces other than New Brunswick shall not be subject to such Dues.

Lumber Dues in New Brunswick.

Exemption of Public Lands, etc.

125. No Lands or Property belonging to Canada or any Province shall be liable to Taxation.

Provincial Consolidated revenue fund.

126. Such Portions of the Duties and Revenues over which the respective Legislatures of Canada, Nova Scotia, and New Brunswick had before the Union Power of Appropriation as are by this Act reserved to the respective Governments or Legislatures of the Provinces, and all Duties and Revenues raised by them in accordance with the special Powers conferred upon them by this Act, shall in each Province form One Consolidated Revenue Fund to be appropriated for the Public Service of the Province.

IX. MISCELLANEOUS PROVISIONS.

General.

As to Legislative Councillors of Provinces becoming senators.

127. If any Person being at the passing of this Act a Member of the Legislative Council of Canada, Nova Scotia, or New Brunswick, to whom a Place in the Senate is offered, does not within Thirty Days thereafter, by Writing under his Hand addressed to the Governor General of the Province of Canada or to the Lieutenant-Governor of Nova Scotia or New Brunswick (as the Case may be), accept the same, he shall be deemed to have declined the same; and any Person who, being at the passing of this Act a Member of the Legislative Council of Nova Scotia or New Brunswick, accepts a Place in the Senate shall thereby vacate his Seat in such Legislative Council.

Oath of Allegiance, etc.

128. Every Member of the Senate or House of Commons of Canada shall before taking his Seat therein take and subscribe before the Governor General or some Person authorized by him, and every Member of a Legislative Council or Legislative Assembly of any Province shall before taking his Seat therein take and subscribe before the Lieutenant-Governor of the Province or some Person authorized by him, the Oath of Allegiance contained in the Fifth Schedule to this Act; and every Member of the Senate of Canada and every Member of the Legislative Council of Quebec shall also, before taking his Seat therein, take and subscribe before the Governor General, or some Person authorized by him, the Declaration of Qualification contained in the same Schedule.

129. Except as otherwise provided by this Act, all Laws in force in Canada, Nova Scotia, or New Brunswick at the Union, and all Courts of Civil and Criminal Jurisdiction, and all legal Commissions, Powers, and Authorities, and all Officers, Judicial, Administrative, and Ministerial, existing therein at the Union, shall continue in Ontario, Quebec, Nova Scotia, and New Brunswick respectively, as if the Union had not been made; subject nevertheless (except with respect to such as are enacted by or exist under Acts of the Parliament of Great Britain or of the Parliament of the United Kingdom of Great Britain and Ireland,) to be repealed, abolished, or altered by the Parliament of Canada, or by the Legislature of the respective Province, according to the Authority of the Parliament or of that Legislature under this Act. Continuance of existing Laws, Courts, Officers, etc.

130. Until the Parliament of Canada otherwise provides, all Officers of the several Provinces having Duties to discharge in relation to Matters other than those coming within the Classes of Subjects by this Act assigned exclusively to the Legislatures of the Provinces shall be Officers of Canada, and shall continue to discharge the Duties of their respective Offices under the same Liabilities, Responsibilities, and Penalties as if the Union had not been made. Transfer of officers to Canada.

131. Until the Parliament of Canada otherwise provides, the Governor General in Council may from Time to Time appoint such Officers as the Governor General in Council deems necessary or proper for the effectual Execution of this Act. Appointment of new officers.

132. The Parliament and Government of Canada shall have all Powers necessary or proper for performing the Obligations of Canada or of any Province thereof, as Part of the British Empire, towards Foreign Countries, arising under Treaties between the Empire and such Foreign Countries. Treaty obligations.

133. Either the English or the French Language may be used by any Person in the Debates of the Houses of the Parliament of Canada and of the Houses of the Legislature of Quebec; and Use of English and French Languages.

both those Languages shall be used in the respective Records and Journals of those Houses; and either of those Languages may be used by any Person or in any Pleading or Process in or issuing from any Court of Canada established under this Act, and in or from all or any of the Courts of Quebec.

The Acts of the Parliament of Canada and of the Legislature of Quebec shall be printed and published in both those Languages.

Ontario and Quebec.

134. Until the Legislature of Ontario or of Quebec otherwise provides, the Lieutenant-Governors of Ontario and Quebec may each appoint under the Great Seal of the Province the following Officers, to hold Office during Pleasure, that is to say,—the Attorney-General, the Secretary and Registrar of the Province, the Treasurer of the Province, the Commissioner of Crown Lands, and the Commissioner of Agriculture and Public Works, and in the Case of Quebec the Solicitor General, and may, by Order of the Lieutenant-Governor in Council, from Time to Time prescribe the Duties of those Officers and of the several Departments over which they shall preside or to which they shall belong, and of the Officers and Clerks thereof; and may also appoint other and additional Officers to hold Office during Pleasure, and may from Time to Time prescribe the Duties of those Officers, and of the several Departments over which they shall preside or to which they shall belong, and of the Officers and Clerks thereof.

135. Until the Legislature of Ontario or Quebec otherwise provides, all Rights, Powers, Duties, Functions, Responsibilities, or Authorities at the passing of this Act vested in or imposed on the Attorney-General, Solicitor General, Secretary and Registrar of the Province of Canada, Minister of Finance, Commissioner of Crown Lands, Commissioner of Public Works, and Minister of Agriculture and Receiver General, by any Law, Statute or Ordinance of Upper Canada, Lower Canada, or Canada, and not repugnant to this Act, shall be vested in or imposed on any Officer to be appointed by the Lieutenant-

Governor for the Discharge of the same or any of them; and the Commissioner of Agriculture and Public Works shall perform the Duties and Functions of the Office of Minister of Agriculture at the passing of this Act imposed by the Law of the Province of Canada, as well as those of the Commissioner of Public Works.

136. Until altered by the Lieutenant-Governor in Council, the Great Seals of Ontario and Quebec respectively shall be the same, or of the same Design, as those used in the Provinces of Upper Canada and Lower Canada respectively before their Union as the Province of Canada. Great Seals.

137. The Words "and from thence to the End of the then next ensuing Session of the Legislature," or Words to the same Effect, used in any temporary Act of the Province of Canada not expired before the Union, shall be construed to extend and apply to the next Session of the Parliament of Canada if the subject Matter of the Act is within the Powers of the same, as defined by this Act, or to the next Sessions of the Legislatures of Ontario and Quebec respectively if the Subject Matter of the Act is within the Powers of the same as defined by this Act. Construction of temporary Acts.

138. From and after the Union the Use of the Words "Upper Canada" instead of "Ontario," or "Lower Canada" instead of "Quebec," in any Deed, Writ, Process, Pleading, Document, Matter, or Thing, shall not invalidate the same. As to Errors in Names.

139. Any Proclamation under the Great Seal of the Province of Canada issued before the Union to take effect at a Time which is subsequent to the Union, whether relating to that Province, or to Upper Canada, or to Lower Canada, and the several Matters and Things therein proclaimed shall be and continue of like Force and Effect as if the Union had not been made. As to issue of Proclamations before Union, to commence after Union.

140. Any Proclamation which is authorized by any Act of the Legislature of the Province of Canada to be issued under the Great Seal of the Province of Canada, whether relating to that Province, or to Upper Canada, or to Lower Canada, and which is not issued before the Union, may be issued by the As to issue of Proclamations after Union.

Lieutenant-Governor of Ontario or of Quebec, as its Subject Matter requires, under the Great Seal thereof; and from and after the Issue of such Proclamation the same and the several Matters and Things therein proclaimed shall be and continue of the like Force and Effect in Ontario or Quebec as if the Union had not been made.

<small>Penitentiary.</small> **141.** The Penitentiary of the Province of Canada shall, until the Parliament of Canada otherwise provides, be and continue the Penitentiary of Ontario and of Quebec.

<small>Arbitration respecting debts, etc.</small> **142.** The Division and Adjustment of the Debts, Credits, Liabilities, Properties, and Assets of Upper Canada and Lower Canada shall be referred to the Arbitrament of Three Arbitrators, One chosen by the Government of Ontario, One by the Government of Quebec, and One by the Government of Canada; and the Selection of the Arbitrators shall not be made until the Parliament of Canada and the Legislatures of Ontario and Quebec have met; and the Arbitrator chosen by the Government of Canada shall not be a Resident either in Ontario or in Quebec.

<small>Division of records.</small> **143.** The Governor General in Council may from Time to Time order that such and so many of the Records, Books, and Documents of the Province of Canada as he thinks fit shall be appropriated and delivered either to Ontario or to Quebec, and the same shall thenceforth be the Property of that Province; and any Copy thereof or Extract therefrom, duly certified by the Officer having charge of the Original thereof, shall be admitted as Evidence.

<small>Constitution of townships in Quebec.</small> **144.** The Lieutenant-Governor of Quebec may from Time to Time, by Proclamation under the Great Seal of the Province, to take effect from a day to be appointed therein, constitute Townships in those Parts of the Province of Quebec in which Townships are not then already constituted, and fix the Metes and Bounds thereof.

X. INTERCOLONIAL RAILWAY.

<small>Duty of Government and Parliament of</small> **145.** Inasmuch as the Provinces of Canada, Nova Scotia, and New Brunswick have joined in a Declaration that the Construc-

tion of the Intercolonial Railway is essential to the Consolidation of the Union of British North America, and to the Assent thereto of Nova Scotia and New Brunswick, and have consequently agreed that Provision should be made for its immediate Construction by the Government of Canada: Therefore, in order to give effect to that Agreement, it shall be the Duty of the Government and Parliament of Canada to provide for the Commencement within Six Months after the Union, of a Railway connecting the River St. Lawrence with the City of Halifax in Nova Scotia, and for the Construction thereof without Intermission, and the Completion thereof with all practicable Speed.

Canada to make Railway herein described.

XI. ADMISSION OF OTHER COLONIES.

146. It shall be lawful for the Queen, by and with the Advice of Her Majesty's Most Honourable Privy Council, on Addresses from the Houses of the Parliament of Canada, and from the Houses of the respective Legislatures of the Colonies or Provinces of Newfoundland, Prince Edward Island, and British Columbia, to admit those Colonies or Provinces, or any of them, into the Union, and on Address from the Houses of the Parliament of Canada to admit Rupert's Land and the North-western Territory, or either of them, into the Union, on such Terms and Conditions in each Case as are in the Addresses expressed and as the Queen thinks fit to approve, subject to the Provisions of this Act; and the Provisions of any Order in Council in that Behalf shall have effect as if they had been enacted by the Parliament of the United Kingdom of Great Britain and Ireland.

Power to admit Newfoundland, etc., into the Union.

*****147.** In case of the Admission of Newfoundland and Prince Edward Island, or either of them, each shall be entitled to a Representation in the Senate of Canada of Four Members, and (notwithstanding anything in this Act) in case of the Admission of Newfoundland the normal Number of Senators shall be Seventy-six and their maximum Number shall be Eighty-two; but Prince Edward Island when admitted shall be deemed to be comprised in the third of the Three Divisions into which Canada is, in relation to the Constitution of the Senate, divided by this Act, and accordingly, after the Admission of Prince Edward

As to Representation of Newfoundland and Prince Edward Island in Senate.

*Altered by 1915 Amendment. See Appendix E.

Island, whether Newfoundland is admitted or not, the Representation of Nova Scotia and New Brunswick in the Senate shall, as Vacancies occur, be reduced from Twelve to Ten Members respectively, and the Representation of each of those Provinces shall not be increased at any Time beyond Ten, *except under the Provision of this Act for the Appointment of Three or Six additional Senators under the Direction of the Queen.

*Altered by 1915 Amendment. See Appendix E.

B. THE BRITISH NORTH AMERICA ACT, 1871

Brit. Statutes, 34-35 Victoria, Chapter 28.

An Act respecting the establishment of Provinces in the Dominion of Canada.

[*29th June, 1871.*]

WHEREAS doubts have been entertained respecting the powers of the Parliament of Canada to establish Provinces in Territories admitted, or which may hereafter be admitted, into the Dominion of Canada, and to provide for the representation of such Provinces in the said Parliament, and it is expedient to remove such doubts, and to vest such powers in the said Parliament:

Be it enacted by the Queen's Most Excellent Majesty, by and with the advice and consent of the Lords Spiritual and Temporal, and Commons, in this present Parliament assembled, and by the authority of the same, as follows:—

1. This Act may be cited for all purposes as The British North America Act, 1871. Short title.

2. The Parliament of Canada may from time to time establish new Provinces in any territories forming for the time being part of the Dominion of Canada, but not included in any Province thereof, and may, at the time of such establishment, make provision for the constitution and administration of any such Province, and for the passing of laws for the peace, order, and good government of such Province, and for its representation in the said Parliament. Parliament of Canada may establish new Provinces and provide for the constitution, etc., thereof.

3. The Parliament of Canada may from time to time, with the consent of the Legislature of any Province of the said Dominion, increase, diminish, or otherwise alter the limits of such Province, upon such terms and conditions as may be agreed to by the said Legislature, and may, with the like consent, make provision respecting the effect and operation of any such increase or diminution or alteration of territory in relation to any Province affected thereby. Alteration of limits of Provinces.

4. The Parliament of Canada may from time to time make provision for the administration, peace, order, and good government of any territory not for the time being included in any Province.

<small>Parliament of Canada may legislate for any territory not included in a Province.</small>

5. The following Acts passed by the said Parliament of Canada, and intituled respectively,—"An Act for the temporary government of Rupert's Land and the North Western Territory when united with Canada"; and "An Act to amend and continue the Act thirty-two and thirty-three Victoria, chapter three, and to establish and provide for the government of "the Province of Manitoba," shall be and be deemed to have been valid and effectual for all purposes whatsoever from the date at which they respectively received the assent, in the Queen's name, of the Governor General of the said Dominion of Canada.

<small>Confirmation of Acts of Parliament of Canada, 32 & 33 Vict., (Canadian) cap. 3, 33 Vict., (Canadian) cap. 3.</small>

6. Except as provided by the third section of this Act, it shall not be competent for the Parliament of Canada to alter the provisions of the last-mentioned Act of the said Parliament in so far as it relates to the Province of Manitoba, or of any other Act hereafter establishing new Provinces in the said Dominion, subject always to the right of the Legislature of the Province of Manitoba to alter from time to time the provisions of any law respecting the qualification of electors and members of the Legislative Assembly, and to make laws respecting elections in the said Province.

<small>Limitation of powers of Parliament of Canada to legislate for an established Province.</small>

C. THE PARLIAMENT OF CANADA ACT, 1875

Brit. Statutes, 38-39 Victoria, Chapter 38.

An Act to remove certain doubts with respect to the powers of the Parliament of Canada under Section Eighteen of the British North America Act, 1867.

[*19th July, 1875.*]

WHEREAS by section eighteen of the British North America Act, 1867, it is provided as follows: "The privileges, immunities, and powers to be held, enjoyed, and exercised by the Senate and by the House of Commons, and by the Members thereof respectively, shall be such as are from time to time defined by Act of the Parliament of Canada, but so that the same shall never exceed those at the passing of this Act held, enjoyed, and exercised by the Commons House of Parliament of the United Kingdom of Great Britain and Ireland, and by the Members thereof:" <small>30 & 31 Vict., c. 3.</small>

And whereas doubts have arisen with regard to the power of defining by an Act of the Parliament of Canada, in pursuance of the said section, the said privileges, powers, or immunities; and it is expedient to remove such doubts:

Be it therefore enacted by the Queen's Most Excellent Majesty, by and with, the advice and consent of the Lords Spiritual and Temporal, and Commons, in this present Parliament assembled, and by the authority of the same, as follows:—

1. Section eighteen of the British North America Act, 1867, is hereby repealed, without prejudice to anything done under that section, and the following section shall be substituted for the section so repealed. <small>Substitution of new section for section 18 of 30 & 31 Vict., c. 3.</small>

The privileges, immunities, and powers to be held, enjoyed, and exercised by the Senate and by the House of Commons, and by the members thereof respectively, shall be such as are from time to time defined by Act of the Parliament of Canada, but so that any Act of the Parliament of Canada defining such privileges, immunities, and powers shall not confer any privileges, immunities, or powers exceeding those at the passing of such Act held, enjoyed, and exercised by the Commons House of Parliament of the United Kingdom of Great Britain and Ireland, and by the Members thereof.

Confirmation of Act of Parliament of Canada 31 & 32 Vict., c. 24.

2. The Act of the Parliament of Canada passed in the thirty-first year of the reign of Her present Majesty, chapter twenty-four intituled "An Act to provide for oaths to witnesses being administered in certain cases for the purposes of either House of Parliament," shall be deemed to be valid, and to have been valid as from the date at which the Royal Assent was given thereto by the Governor General of the Dominion of Canada.

Short title.

3. This Act may be cited as the Parliament of Canada Act, 1875.

D. THE BRITISH NORTH AMERICA ACT, 1886

Brit. Statutes, 49-50 Victoria, Chapter 35.

An Act respecting the Representation in the Parliament of Canada of Territories which for the time being form part of the Dominion of Canada, but are not included in any Province.

[*25th June, 1886.*]

WHEREAS it is expedient to empower the Parliament of Canada to provide for the representation in the Senate and House of Commons of Canada, or either of them, of any territory which for the time being forms part of the Dominion of Canada, but is not included in any province:

Be it therefore enacted by the Queen's most Excellent Majesty, by and with the advice and consent of the Lords Spiritual and Temporal, and Commons, in this present Parliament assembled, and by the authority of the same as follows:—

1. The Parliament of Canada may from time to time make provision for the representation in the Senate and House of Commons of Canada, or in either of them, of any territories which for the time being form part of the Dominion of Canada, but are not included in any province thereof. Provision by Parliament of Canada for representation of territories.

2. Any Act passed by the Parliament of Canada before the passing of this Act for the purpose mentioned in this Act shall, if not disallowed by the Queen, be, and shall be deemed to have been, valid and effectual from the date at which it received the assent, in Her Majesty's name, of the Governor General of Canada. Effect of Acts of Parliament of Canada.

It is hereby declared that any Act passed by the Parliament of Canada, whether before or after the passing of this Act, for the purpose mentioned in this Act or in the British North America Act, 1871, has effect, notwithstanding anything in the British North America Act, 1867, and the number of Senators or the number of Members of the House of Commons specified 34 & 35 Vict., c. 28.
30 & 31 Vict., c. 3.

in the last-mentioned Act is increased by the number of Senators or of Members, as the case may be, provided by any such Act of the Parliament of Canada for the representation of any provinces or territories of Canada.

<small>Short title and construction.
30 & 31 Vict., c. 3.
34 & 35 Vict., c. 28.</small>

3. This Act may be cited as the British North America Act, 1886.

This Act and the British North America Act, 1867, and the British North America Act, 1871, shall be construed together, and may be cited together as the British North America Acts, 1867 to 1886.

E. THE BRITISH NORTH AMERICA ACT, 1915

Brit. Statutes, 5-6 George V, Chapter 45.

An Act to amend the British North America Act, 1867.

[*19th May, 1915.*]

Be it enacted by the King's most Excellent Majesty, by and with the advice and consent of the Lords Spiritual and Temporal, and Commons, in this present Parliament assembled, and by the authority of the same, as follows:—

1. (1) Notwithstanding anything in the British North America Act, 1867, or in any Act amending the same, or in any Order in Council or terms or conditions of union made or approved under the said Acts or in any Act of the Canadian Parliament— <small>Alteration of constitution of Senate. 30 and 31 Vict., c. 3.</small>

(i) The number of senators provided for under section twenty-one of the British North America Act, 1867, is increased from seventy-two to ninety-six:

(ii) The Divisions of Canada in relation to the constitution of the Senate provided for by section twenty-two of the said Act are increased from three to four, the Fourth Division to comprise the Western Provinces of Manitoba, British Columbia, Saskatchewan, and Alberta, which four Divisions shall (subject to the provisions of the said Act and of this Act) be equally represented in the Senate, as follows:— Ontario by twenty-four senators; Quebec by twenty-four senators; the Maritime Provinces and Prince Edward Island by twenty-four senators, ten thereof representing Nova Scotia, ten thereof representing New Brunswick, and four thereof representing Prince Edward Island; the Western Provinces by twenty-four senators, six thereof representing Manitoba, six thereof representing British Columbia, six thereof representing Saskatchewan, and six thereof representing Alberta:

(iii) The number of persons whom by section twenty-six of the said Act the Governor General of Canada may, upon the direction of His Majesty the King, add to the Senate is increased from three or six to four or eight, representing equally the four divisions of Canada:

(iv) In case of such addition being at any time made the Governor General of Canada shall not summon any person to the Senate except upon a further like direction by His Majesty the King on the like recommendation to represent one of the four Divisions until such Division is represented by twenty-four senators and no more:

(v) The number of senators shall not at any time exceed one hundred and four:

(vi) The representation in the Senate to which by section one hundred and forty-seven of the British North America Act, 1867, Newfoundland would be entitled in case of its admission to the Union is increased from four to six **members**, and in case of the admission of Newfoundland into the Union, notwithstanding anything in the said Act or in this Act, the normal number of senators shall be one hundred and two, and their maximum number one hundred and ten:

<small>49 and 50 Vict., c. 35.</small> (vii) Nothing herein contained shall affect the powers of the Canadian Parliament under the British North America Act, 1886.

(2) Paragraphs (i) to (vi) inclusive of subsection (1) of this section shall not take affect before the termination of the now existing Canadian Parliament.

<small>Constitution of House of Commons.</small> **2.** The British North America Act, 1867, is amended by adding thereto the following section immediately after section fifty-one of the said Act:—

"**51A.** Notwithstanding anything in this Act a province shall always be entitled to a number of members in the House of Commons not less than the number of senators representing such province."

<small>Short title.</small> **3.** This Act may be cited as the British North America Act, 1915, and the British North America Acts, 1867 to 1886, and this Act may be cited together as the British North America Acts, 1867 to 1915.

F. THE BRITISH NORTH AMERICA ACT, 1940

Brit. Statutes, 3-4 George VI, Chapter 36.

An Act to include Unemployment Insurance among the classes of subjects enumerated in Section Ninety-one of the British North America Act, 1867.

[*10th July, 1940.*]

WHEREAS the Senate and Commons of Canada in Parliament assembled have submitted an address to His Majesty praying that His Majesty may graciously be pleased to cause a Bill to be laid before the Parliament of the United Kingdom for the enactment of the provisions hereinafter set forth:—

Be it therefore enacted by the King's most Excellent Majesty, by and with the advice and consent of the Lords Spiritual and Temporal, and Commons, in this present Parliament assembled, and by the authority of the same, as follows:—

1. Section ninety-one of the British North America Act, 1867, is amended by inserting therein, after item 2 "The regulation of trade and commerce", the following item:— *Extension of exclusive legislative authority of Parliament of Canada. 30 & 31 Vict., c. 3.*

"2A. Unemployment insurance."

2. This Act may be cited as the British North America Act, 1940, and the British North America Acts, 1867 to 1930, the British North America Act, 1907, and this Act may be cited together as the British North America Acts, 1867 to 1940. *Short title and citation 7 Edw. 7 c. 11.*

G. THE BRITISH NORTH AMERICA ACT, 1946

Brit. Statutes, 10 George VI, Chapter 63.

An Act to provide for the readjustment of representation in the House of Commons of Canada on the basis of the population of Canada.

[*26th July, 1946.*]

WHEREAS the Senate and House of Commons in Parliament assembled have submitted an address to His Majesty praying that His Majesty may graciously be pleased to cause a Bill to be laid before the Parliament of the United Kingdom for the enactment of the provisions hereinafter set forth;

Be it therefore enacted by the King's most Excellent Majesty, by and with the advice and consent of the Lords Spiritual and Temporal, and Commons, in this present Parliament assembled, and by the authority of the same, as follows:

<small>New provision as to readjustment of representation in Commons. 30 & 31 Vict., c. 3.</small>

1. Section fifty-one of the British North America Act, 1867, is hereby repealed and the following substituted therefor:

"**51.**—(1) The number of members of the House of Commons shall be two hundred and fifty-five and the representation of the provinces therein shall forthwith upon the coming into force of this section and thereafter on the completion of each decennial census be readjusted by such authority, in such manner, and from such time as the Parliament of Canada from time to time provides, subject and according to the following rules:—

1. Subject as hereinafter provided, there shall be assigned to each of the provinces a number of members computed by dividing the total population of the provinces by two hundred and fifty-four and by dividing the population of each province by the quotient so obtained, disregarding, except as hereinafter in this section provided, the remainder, if any, after the said process of division.

2. If the total number of members assigned to all the provinces pursuant to rule one is less than two hundred and fifty-

four, additional members shall be assigned to the provinces (one to a province) having remainders in the computation under rule one commencing with the province having the largest remainder and continuing with the other provinces in the order of the magnitude of their respective remainders until the total number of members assigned is two hundred and fifty-four.

3. Notwithstanding anything in this section, if upon completion of a computation under rules one and two, the number of members to be assigned to a province is less than the number of senators representing the said province, rules one and two shall cease to apply in respect of the said province, and there shall be assigned to the said province a number of members equal to the said number of senators.

4. In the event that rules one and two cease to apply in respect of a province then, for the purpose of computing the number of members to be assigned to the provinces in respect of which rules one and two continue to apply, the total population of the provinces shall be reduced by the number of the population of the province in respect of which rules one and two have ceased to apply and the number two hundred and fifty-four shall be reduced by the number of members assigned to such province pursuant to rule three.

5. Such readjustment shall not take effect until the termination of the then existing Parliament.

(2) The Yukon Territory as constituted by Chapter forty-one of the Statutes of Canada, 1901, together with any Part of Canada not comprised within a province which may from time to time be included therein by the Parliament of Canada for the purposes of representation in Parliament, shall be entitled to one member."

2. This Act may be cited as the British North America Act, 1946, and the British North America Acts, 1867 to 1943, and this Act may be cited together as the British North America Acts, 1867 to 1946. *Short title and citation.*

H. THE BRITISH NORTH AMERICA ACT, 1949

Brit. Statutes, 12-13 George VI, Chapter 22.

An Act to confirm and give effect to Terms of Union agreed between Canada and Newfoundland.

[*A.D. 1949.*]

WHEREAS by means of a referendum the people of Newfoundland have by a majority signified their wish to enter into confederation with Canada;

And whereas the Agreement containing Terms of Union between Canada and Newfoundland set out in the Schedule to this Act has been duly approved by the Parliament of Canada and by the Government of Newfoundland;

And whereas Canada has requested, and consented to, the enactment of an Act of the Parliament of the United Kingdom to confirm and give effect to the said Agreement, and the Senate and House of Commons of Canada in Parliament assembled have submitted an address to His Majesty praying that His Majesty may graciously be pleased to cause a Bill to be laid before the Parliament of the United Kingdom for that purpose:

Be it therefore enacted by the King's most Excellent Majesty by and with the advice and consent of the Lords Spiritual and Temporal and Commons in this present Parliament assembled and by the authority of the same, as follows:

<small>Confirmation of terms of Union</small>

1. The Agreement containing Terms of Union between Canada and Newfoundland set out in the Schedule to this Act is hereby confirmed and shall have the force of law notwithstanding anything in the British North America Acts, 1867 to 1946.

<small>Repeal of 24 & 25 Geo. 5 c. 2.</small>

2. In accordance with the preceding section the provisions of the Newfoundland Act, 1933, other than section three thereof (which relates to guarantee of certain securities of Newfoundland) shall be repealed as from the coming into force of the said Terms of Union.

3. This Act may be cited as the British North America Act, 1949, and the British North America Acts, 1867 to 1946, and this Act may be cited together as the British North America Acts, 1867 to 1949. *Short title and citation*

Bibliography

GENERAL STUDIES

BRADY, A. *Canada*. Toronto: The Macmillan Company, 1932.
———. *Democracy in the Dominions*. Toronto: University of Toronto Press, 1947.
CLOKIE, H. McD. *Canadian Government and Politics*. Toronto: Longmans Green & Co., 1944.
CORRY, J. A. *Democratic Government and Politics*. Toronto: University of Toronto Press, 1946.
CREIGHTON, D. G. *Dominion of the North*. Boston: Houghton-Mifflin Company, 1944.
DAWSON, R. MACG. *Constitutional Issues in Canada, 1900-31*. London: Oxford University Press, 1933.
———. *The Development of Dominion Status, 1900-36*. London: Oxford University Press, 1937.
———. *The Government of Canada*. Toronto: University of Toronto Press, 1947.
LOWER, A. R. M. *Colony to Nation*. Toronto: Longmans Green & Co., 1946.

SPECIAL STUDIES AND SOURCES

BEAUCHESNE, A. (Editor). *Rules and Forms of the House of Commons of Canada*. Toronto: Canada Law Book Co., 1943.
COLE, TAYLOR. *The Canadian Bureaucracy*. Durham, N.C.: Duke University Press, 1949.
DAWSON, R. MACG. *The Civil Service of Canada*. London: Oxford University Press, 1929.
FORSEY, E. A. *The Royal Power of Dissolution of Parliament in the British Commonwealth*. Toronto: Oxford University Press, 1943.
GETTYS, C. L. *The Administration of Canadian Conditional Grants*. Chicago: Public Administration Service, 1938.
KENNEDY, W. P. M. *The Constitution of Canada*. London: Oxford University Press, 1938.
LANGSTONE, ROSA W. *Responsible Government in Canada*. London: J. M. Dent & Sons, Ltd., 1941.

MacKay, R. A. *The Unreformed Senate of Canada*. Oxford: University Press, 1926.

Maxwell, J. A. *Federal Subsidies to the Provincial Governments in Canada.* Cambridge: Harvard University Press, 1937.

Trotter, R. G. *Canadian Federation.* Toronto: J. M. Dent & Sons, Ltd., 1924.

Whitelaw, W. M. *The Maritimes and Canada before Confederation.* Toronto: Oxford University Press, 1934.

The Canadian Journal of Economics and Political Science, 1935 *et seq.* Toronto: University of Toronto Press.

Proceedings, Canadian Political Science Association, 1913, 1930-34. Kingston: The Jackson Press.

Official Reports

British North America Acts and Selected Statutes, 1867-1948. Ottawa: Printer to the King, 1949.

Proposals of the Government of Canada (Dominion-Provincial Conference on Reconstruction). Ottawa: Printer to the King, 1945.

Report of the Royal Commission on Dominion-Provincial Relations (Rowell-Sirois Report). Ottawa: Printer to the King, 1938-39.

Report on the British North America Act (Senate of Canada) (O'Connor Report). Ottawa: Printer to the King, 1939.

Index

Alberta, 6n, 9n, 12, 18, 63, 65, 73, 113, 114, 115, 126
amendment, *see* British North America Act
Aristotle, 3
assent, refusal of, 105
Athens, democracy in, 5
Auditor-General, 84
autonomy, Canadian, 14-16, 37-38

Bill of rights, *see* civil liberties
bills: classification of, 48-49; government, 48-50; money, 66, 67; passage of, 62, 65, 80-82; private, 48-49, 65-67; private member, 48-49, 79; public, 48, 80-82
boards, *see* commissions
Borden, Sir R. L., 66
Bowell Cabinet, 45
British Columbia, 6n, 9n, 12, 33n, 43, 63, 73, 114, 117n, 124
British Commonwealth, 14-16
British North America Act, 11, 17-18, 19-20, 25-30, 66, 96, 98, 103, 104, 116: amendment of, 15, 19-20, 22-24, 71; amendments, 30n, 63, 72, 73, 76; distribution of power, *see* distribution of power; financial provisions, *see* Dominion-provincial relations; interpretation of, 20-22, 27-30, 95; omissions in, 18, 22, 41
budget, 83-84, 88
by-elections, 74

Cabinet, 41-50, 65, 85-94: character of, 41-42; civil service and, 46, 51-52, 55, 90-91; composition, 41-42; early examples, 6-9; financial powers, 50, 82-84, 85; functions, 19, 46-50, 85; Governor-General and, 22, 37-40, 62; House of Commons, relation to 6-9, 18-19, 69-71, 78-80, 85-94; Ministers, 44-47, 51-52, 56, 63, 75, 128; personnel, 42-44; position of, 19, 44-46; representative character, 43-44; responsibility, 6-9, 18-19, 44, 52, 55, 85; Senate, relation to, 66-67, 68
Canada, province of, 10, 11
Canadian Broadcasting Corporation, 51, 61
Canadian government, characteristics of, 3-16
caucus, party, 45
Charlottetown Conference, 10
civil liberties, 12-14, 21
civil service, *see* departments, 51-61: administration, 53-56; Cabinet and, 46, 51-52, 55, 90-91; delegated powers, exercise of, 53-56; dismissals, 53; entrance, 52-53; functions, 51-52; patronage, 52-53; reform, 53; tenure, 53
Civil Service Commission, 52, 60
closure, 79
Commission, Royal, *see* Royal Commission
commissions, 60-61
Committee: select, 46, 81; stage, 80-82; standing, 81
Committee of Supply, *see* Supply
Committee of Ways and Means, *see* Ways and Means
Committee of Whole, 81-82
common law, 21
Communist party, see Labour-Progressive p rty
compact theory, 22-23
Comptroller of Treasury, 57, 84
concurrent powers, 27
Confederation, 10n, 10-12
Conference: Charlottetown, 10; Dominion-provincial, 34-35; Imperial, 15, 38; London, 11; Quebec, 10-11
constitution, Canadian, *see* British North America Act, usage, etc. 17-24: Amendment of, 15, 17, 22-24; development of, 21-22; interpretation of, 20-22, 27-30, 95; nature of, 17-21
constitutional statutes, 17-18, 19
convention, *see* usage
convention, party, *see* party

185

Index

Co-operative Commonwealth Federation party, 122, 126, 129
County Court, 97 99
courts, *see* Supreme Court, County Court, etc.: minor, 97; system of, 96-98
custom, *see* usage

Democratic government, 3-5
departments, federal, 56-60; provincial, 107-10
depression, effect of, 34
Dickens, Charles, 102
dictatorships, 4, 13
disallowance, 47, 104
discretionary powers, 12-13, 53-56
dismissal of Ministers, 39-40, 105
dissolution, 40, 47, 47*n*, 85
distribution of power, 9-10, 17, 25-30, 31-36, 104: "aspect" doctrine, 28; complexity of, 27-28; concurrent powers, 27; Dominion powers, 9-10, 20, 25-26, 28-30, 31-36, 96; education, 23-24, 27, 33; emergency powers, 29; finance, 26-28, 30, 31-36; "peace, order, and good government", 25, 29-30, 33; "property and civil rights", 26, 29, 30; provincial powers, 9-10, 20, 23, 26-27, 30, 31-36, 96, 116; residual power, 25, 28-30, 33; results of, 32-36
division of power, 7, 14, 99-100
Dominion-provincial relations, *see* distribution of powers, Conference, disallowance, etc., 31-36, 120, 123
Durham report, 8

education, 23-24, 27, 33, 47, 108, 118
elections, 73-74
Elgin, Lord, 8
emergency powers, 29
estimates, 82-83
Exchequer Court, 97-98
Executive Council, 6, 8-9

federalism, *see* distribution of power
Finance, Minister of, 57, 82-83
finance Dominion-provincial, 26-28, 30, 31-36
financial legislation, 82-84
Foster, Sir George E., 64-65
franchise, 73-74, 112

government activity, growth of, 13, 30, 33, 53-54
Governor, early, 5-6, 8-9, 18, 37
Governor-General, 37-40, 62, 80, 87: appointment of, 38; Cabinet and, 22, 38-40, 62; functions of, 22, 38-40; Lieutenant-Governor, compared to, 104-6; powers of; 19, 37-40, 42
Governor-General-in-Council, 21, 27, 42, 47, 63, 72, 95, 96-100, 104
grants-in-aid, 32, 110
Great Britain, 14-16: influence of, 6-7, 12, 14, 18, 37, 67, 75-76, 102-3, 126; Acts of Parliament of, 15-16, 19-20, 22-24

Halifax, 6, 73
House of Commons, 5, 62, 69-94: Cabinet, relations to, 6-9, 18-19, 69-71, 78-80, 85-94; committees, 46, 81-83; criticism in, 86-89; debate in, 78-82; dissolution, 40, 47, 47*n*, 85; election of, 73-74; elections, controverted, 74; financial powers, 66, 67, 82-84; franchise, 73-74; functions of, 69-72; legislative process, 80-84; nomination for, 74, 127; Opposition in, *see* Opposition; party manoeuvres in, 90-94; private members, 44-46, 47-49, 78-80, 86-89; privilege, *see* Parliament, privilege; qualifications, 75; representation, 72-73; rules, 78-80, 86-90; salary, 75; Senate, relation to, 65-67; term, 75
House of Lords, 67

Ilsley, J. L., 90
Imperial Conference, 15, 38
Imperial relations, 14-16
initiative, 114

Joint address, 71-72, 99
Judicial Committee of the Privy Council, 15, 96
judiciary, *see* courts, Supreme Court of Canada, etc., 95-101: appointment, 96-97, 100-1; compared to other officials, 98-101; functions of, 95-96; independence of, 13-14, 98-101; removal, 71-72, 96-99; retirement, 96-98; rule of law and, 13-14, 55, 95; salary, 100, 100*n*; tenure, 96-98

King, His Majesty the, 37, 38, 39, 40, 42*n*, 47, 62
King, W. L. Mackenzie, 39, 92, 125

Labour-Progressive party, 126
languages, use of English and French, 23-24

Index

Laurier, Sir Wilfrid, 124, 125
legislation, process of, 62, 65, 80-84
Legislative Assembly, 6, 8, 9, 106, 112-15
Legislative Council, 6, 8, 103, 112
Liberal party, 122-24, 128
Liberal-Conservative party, 122-24
liberties, *see* civil liberties
Lieutenant-Governor, 26, 103, 104-6
Lieutenant-Governor-in-Council, 95, 104-6, 111
London Conference (and Resolutions), 11
Lower Canada, *see* Quebec

Majority rights, 4-5
Manitoba, 6*n*, 9*n*, 11, 12, 33*n*, 63, 73, 113
Maritime Provinces, 10, 11, 43, 63, 116, 124
merchant shipping legislation, 19
Minister, *see* Cabinet
minority rights, 4-5
municipal government, 21, 95, 109, 116-20: councils, 5, 117-18; rural, 116, 117-18; special bodies, 118-19; taxation, 117, 118, 119, 120; urban, 116-17
Macdonald, Sir John A., 125
Mackenzie Territory, 72, 73

New Brunswick, 6*n*, 9*n*, 10, 11, 33*n*, 63, 73
Newfoundland, 6, 6*n*, 9*n*, 10, 11, 12, 27, 36, 63, 73, 116
North West Territories, 6*n*, 9*n*, 72, 73
Nova Scotia, 6, 6*n*, 9*n*, 10, 11, 18, 33*n*, 63, 73, 97

Ontario, 6*n*, 9*n*, 10, 17, 33*n*, 35-36, 43, 63, 73, 97, 107, 117, 124, 127
Opposition: caucus, 45; functions of, 70-71, 79-80, 90-94; Leader of, 38, 75, 77, 88, 89, 91; opportunities for criticism by, 86-89
orders-in-council, 21, 42, 50, 106

pairing of members, 80*n*
Parliament, *see* House of Commons, Senate, 19: joint address by, 71-72, 99; privileges of, 21, 75-76
parliamentary assistants, 42, 44
parties, political, *see also* Liberal, Liberal-Conservative, etc., 113, 121-29; caucus, 45; conventions, 127-29; distinction between, 122-25; functions of, 44-45, 47-48, 121-22; House of Commons, in, 44-45, 47-48; leader, choice of, 127-29; major, 122-25; minor, 113-14, 125-26; organization, 113, 126-29; patronage, 45, 111-12; platform, 124-25; two party system, 122
plebiscite, 114
Prairie Provinces, 124
preferential vote, 113
Premier, 106-110
Prime Minister, 19, 38-40, 42-46, 47, 63, 75, 77
Prince Edward Island, 6*n*, 9*n*, 10, 11, 12, 33*n*, 36, 63, 72, 73, 112-13, 116
privilege, *see* Parliament
Privy Council, 41-42-44; Judicial Committee of, *see* Judicial Committee
Progressive party, 122, 125-26
Progressive Conservative party, *see* Liberal-Conservative party
proportional representation, 113
prorogation, 47, 47*n*, 85
provinces, economic inequality of, 33-34
provincial government, 102-15: British North America Act and, 22-24; Cabinet, 106-7, 111-12; civil service, 111-12; constitution, 103-4; departments, 107-11; disallowance, 47, 104; finance, *see* finance; legislature, 5, 112-15; Lieutenant-Governor, *see* Lieutenant-Governor; municipal government, *see* municipal government; municipal relations with, 119-20; parties in, 113-14; powers of, 26-30, 31-36, 96; reservation of bills, 47, 104-5; similarity to other governments, 102-3.

Quebec, 5, 6*n*, 9*n*, 10-11, 17, 23, 33*n*, 35-36, 43, 63, 73, 107, 112, 117, 123-24, 126
Quebec Conference (and Resolutions) 10-11
question hour, 87

Rebellion Losses Bill, 8
recall, 114-15
referendum, 114
representation, *see* House of Commons
representative government, 5-6
reservation of bills, 47, 104-5
responsible government, 6-9
Rowell-Sirois report, 34-35
Royal Commission, 46, 105-6
rule of law, 12-13, 55, 95

St. Laurent, L. S., 39
Saskatchewan, 6*n*, 9*n*, 12, 18, 63, 73

select committee, 46, 81
Senate, 62-68: age, 64-65; appointment, 63-65; Cabinet's relations with, 66-67, 68; deadlock provision, 63; functions, 65-68; Government Leader in, 42, 43, 66; House of Commons, relation to, 65-67; investigations by, 66, 67; legislative activity, 65-68, 80; Ministers in, 66-67; party character, 63-64; powers of, 62, 66; privilege, *see* Parliament; purpose of creation, 62; reform, 68; representation in, 62-63, 65; salary, 63
Social Credit party, 126
social services, 13, 30, 32-33, 34*n*, 35-36, 68, 110, 123
Speaker, Mr., 77-78, 89
Speech from the Throne, 87
standing committee, 81
Statute of Westminster, 15, 20, 123
subsidies, *see* finance, grants-in-aid
summoning Parliament, 40, 47, 47*n*, 85
supply, 48, 49, 82-83
Supply, Committee of, 82-83, 88
Supreme Court of Canada, 19, 74, 95, 96-97, 98, 99
Supreme Courts of provinces, 95, 97, 98, 99
Switzerland, 5

Taxation, *see* finance: bills, 48, 49, 50, 83-84; direct, 26-27, 28, 31, 32; federal, 26-27, 32, 34; indirect, 26-27; municipal, 117, 118, 119, 120; provincial, 26-27, 31-32, 34
Transport Commission, 60
Treasury Board, 57, 82, 82*n*
Tweedsmuir, Lord, 4

Unemployment insurance, 30, 30*n*
Union Nationale party, 126
union of powers, 6-7, 14
unitary government, 9, 10
United States, 5, 7, 10, 38; influence of, 11, 62, 128-29
Upper Canada, *see* Ontario
"urgent public importance", 87-88
usage, 9, 17, 18-19, 21-22, 76

Virginia, 6

want of confidence, vote of, 88, 106
war, constitutional effects of, 15-16, 29, 35; declaration of, 15, 72
Ways and Means, 48, 49, 50; Committee of, 83, 88
Westminster, *see* Statute of Westminster
whips, 79

Yukon, 72, 73

DATE DUE

OCT 11